JC QUINTANA

Speaking Frankly About

Customer Relationship Management

Why Customer Relationship Management Is Still Alive And Vital To Your Company's Customer Strategy

Printed in the United States of America.

Speaking Frankly About Customer Relationship Management:
Why Customer Relationship Management Is Still Alive
And Vital To Your Company's Customer Strategy

CRG PRESS®

Kennesaw, Georgia. United States

ISBN 978-0-9889145-1-3 (pbk.)

ISBN 978-0-9889145-3-7 (hc.)

ISBN 978-0-9889145-7-5 (ebook)

6th Edition June 2016

For

My wife Shelley...
Thank you for your amazing
support.

My kids, Reina, Nathaniel,
Jonathan, Michael, and
Adriana ... The Mom, The
Philosopher, The Musician, The
Athlete, and
The Princess.

My Grandkids, Bre and Alex,
your future is so bright.

CONTENTS

FOREWORD i

INTRODUCTION: Speaking Frankly 1

PART ONE

SECTION 1: Speaking About Unification 19

SECTION 2: Speaking About the Acronym 45

SECTION 3: Speaking About Collaboration 73

SECTION 4: Speaking About Resolution 103

SECTION 5: Speaking About Relationships......... 122

SECTION 6: Speaking About Interactions 146

SECTION 7: Speaking About the Customer 167

PART TWO

SECTION 8: Speaking About CRM Tools 181

SECTION 9: Speaking About Industry................. 199

SECTION 10: Speaking About The Journey 209

REFERENCES 219

INDEX   222

SPECIAL ACKNOWLEDGEMENTS 227

FOREWORD

"All sales are relationship sales." This pearl of wisdom has long been known and intuitively understood by successful sales people. That is, the features and benefits (and price) of a company's products are less important than the relationship the prospective customer/ client has with the company, and especially with individuals ("real people") who represent the company. The primacy of relationship over attributes of offered products and services occurs even in "virtual" enterprises in which clients and customers may never even meet, see, or speak to a "real person" in the company, ever more common in our internet age. A relationship nevertheless exists and its quality is of vital importance to the enterprise's commercial success.

Herein, JC Quintana extends this principle more broadly to include all relationships that constitute a corporation's presence in the minds of everyone who experiences interactions with it and its representatives, internally and externally. (It's worth noting that his affectionate dedication to his children and wife in the front matter of this volume indicates that JC "walks the talk" in his personal, as well as his professional, life. The dedication oozes respect and mutual trust, the essential "stuff" of successful relationships in any sector of life.)

Readers will recognize the depth and breadth of JC's knowledge and intuitive understanding of corporate relationship management, drawn from his extensive career experience in the real world of business. His professional success in the CRM industry testifies to his qualifications for writing this book, a vehicle for sharing his wisdom with others.

Dr. Dan Dana, Ph.D.

Educator and author in the field of workplace conflict management and mediation and Founder of the *Mediation Training Institute International.*

Several years ago, around the time when some people fretted over Y2K, I realized that my coveted method of keeping track of Very Important People had to go. Yes, I was proud of the cascading list of names, neatly nested within columns and rows on my spreadsheet. Names with color-coded priorities assigned to them, telling me what I needed to do. Many were blue (it's cool, no need to worry). Others were shouting at me in bold red (do something!). My favorites were green: paying clients.

I had done very well with my lists until the day someone introduced me to the concept of CRM. It was the early days of these nascent technologies and companies like mine began to experiment with CRM tools. As I began to use my first CRM software, I remember at first being intimidated by its complexity. But I soon became so enamored by its organizational power, that I forgot the reason it had been suggested to me in the first place. I now had a bigger and better toolkit, and I was playing with my tools. My first attempt at CRM was what one would call a Failed Implementation.

This book makes the seemingly straightforward argument that CRM is about relationships and the value that you place on them. In the traditional sense, CRM is very much like a better mousetrap than my color-coded spreadsheets; all about the customer (the first C in CRM) and improving how you manage that relationship.

You may have guessed that the person who introduced me to CRM was JC Quintana. JC understands that people like me — traditional users of CRM software — have a narrower view about what CRM is and what it can do. To many of us. CRM is a means to keeping track of people, typically defined as customers and prospects, but that is a very limited interpretation of the value of CRM.

In JC's world, those "people" extend beyond customers and prospects to employees, vendors, suppliers, and others. All the stakeholders in the system are connected in one way or another. Consequently, a truly empowered CRM vision, fully embraced by an organization, can lead to more profound connections among all stakeholders. A robust CRM system is designed to help a company be better equipped to fulfill the needs of everyone involved, from client to coworker. When everyone is a part of the solution, the level of commitment by everyone is strengthened across the organization.

This worldview is less transactional than the common take on CRM; instead, it underlies a holistic approach to how a company should operate. In my view, this framework leads to better decision-making by everyone involved. Customers are better informed about what they're buying and with whom they are dealing. Employees have an intrinsic interest in meeting their commitments to both customers and their peers. A holistic approach to CRM has built-in accountability at all levels. The result: a shared sense of purpose and increased levels of trust among all stakeholders.

About a decade ago, when JC and I worked together, I was steadfastly studying and writing about the idea of accountability in the workplace. Following the collapse of Arthur Andersen, Enron, WorldCom and others, people were calling for better accountability from corporate America — the end result being the infamous Sarbanes-Oxley Act of 2002 that set new standards and enforcement for publicly traded companies and public accounting firms. The goal of the legislation, in part, was to restore trust in American business.

Five years after its implementation, our economic system was on the verge of collapse by another group of bad actors in the commercial banking and investments sector. The Dodd-Frank Wall Street and Consumer Protection Act was the response, imposing new rules and regulations on the financial services industry and the regulatory agencies responsible for oversight. Again, the goal was to provide a framework to restore trust and accountability in these institutions.

In a way, a good CRM system functions like Sarbanes-Oxley and Dodd-Frank, but without the punitive intent. It works in the background helping people play by a set of rules that produces a better outcome. Soon, stakeholders make decisions with better information and begin to work collaboratively. Increased accountability and trust are by-products of the system. If you want to understand why this happens, and more importantly, how to build the foundation for such a system, this book is for you.

When I first met JC we had lofty goals about how businesses should be run. We would talk for hours about the company I had and the new company that we were building. We used weighty words like integrity and accountability. We considered our purpose in business and in life and where the two traversed. But we also believed that work should be fun, that work should bring joy to our lives and the others around us. I still feel that way and JC does too.

If you are lucky enough to meet JC one day, you'll see that he is often beaming from ear to ear. You will be struck by his joyful presence. You will know that he cares. I know that this book has been a labor of love. His passion leaps off the page and demands your attention.

This book is an expression of his optimism, a call-to-action for companies not to be great, but to be exceptional. I welcome you to actualize JC's vision, set forth on these pages, within your organization and beyond.

John Marchica
Author of *The Accountable Organization*

INTRODUCTION

SPEAKING ABOUT CHANGE

THE CASE FOR A CRM MANIFESTO.

man·i·fes·to \ noun \ˌma-nə-ˈfes-(ˌ)tō\ :
a written statement declaring publicly the
intentions, motives, or views of
its issuer[1]

"Make the Revolution a parent of settlement, and not a nursery of future revolutions."

– Edmund Burke

Tensions had been running high for two weeks before the events that brought the project to its knees. We sat together in the executive conference room, never used for this project before, only the buzzing fan of a video projector broke the silence. On one side of the table sat the project manager and the leadership team of my company (hired to implement the technology). Next to them sat the IT director and three senior members of another company who had helped build the vision of customer relationship strategy for sales and customer service. On the other side of the table sat three people I had never met before and the manager of the inbound call center. I sat in the corner, anxious, curious. I knew things had not been going as expected, and this was a clear sign that something needed addressing immediately.

One of the people I had not recognized earlier spoke up. He looked directly at the IT director and said:

"I will just come out and state the obvious. We are not happy, and we are not leaving this room until you do something about it."

What came next I can only describe as an explosion of words and angry sentiment from both sides that at times would seem to approach a resolution before taking a turn in an even more frantic direction. For the first time in an endeavor already six months in progress, the people creating a vision of customer relationship management strategy and the people expected to implement it were meeting face-to-face. The goal was to define the impact this effort would have on their business, work life and the customer, yet none of them had spoken once about it together.

In the years since that meeting, I have been a part of many just like it. I usually sit in a different corner: an advocate corner. An advocate for both sides, struggling desperately to define the processes that will help them serve customers better. An advocate for the validity of the needs both sides have for clearer visibility across all areas of the business. What I see from that corner still makes me anxious and more eager than ever to work with people for whom customer relationship management (CRM) is foundational to their business. The view from that corner is of business owners and managers trying to discover the best ways to run their businesses through accurate reporting and management of the pipeline that infuses it. It is of managers trying to improve on the methods that help give customers the products and services they need, while caring for the work life and work environment of people working long hours to succeed together. The landscape is of people genuinely concerned about the happiness and satisfaction of clients and the improvement of their quality of life. To them, it is not just about selling, marketing or customer care. It is about connecting the elderly with the right caregiver; it is about matching a low-income family with the correct programs; it is about helping law enforcement establish a reliable database of offenders. But in the process of designing strategies for improvement, CRM becomes something else altogether.

It becomes a "thing"; a technology. It becomes a cold initiative that stops taking into account that the very components of its name are about people and relationships and managing the moments of significance and human connection that make it what it really is: Customer RELATIONSHIP Management. In its falling away from a relationship building practice, the people charged for its definition and those tasked with its execution stop working together. They become two factions holding close to their belief that one side does not understand the other. One side struggles to learn about their best customers and the practices that lead to increased sales. The other resents being excluded from decisions that could make it more difficult for them to do their job. Both sides look across that conference table with concerns that affect more than just business initiatives, sales opportunities, marketing campaigns, or customer service programs. They affect the lives of real people in a real world.

My role as a corporate relationship advocate (one who advocates that everyone who supports the customer must work together as parts of a collective effort) brings me to this tragic scene often too late. Like a triage nurse, I have to decide which areas are too far-gone and which require immediate attention. It can be discouraging knowing that these mistakes disconnect the strategy from its beneficiary, the customer from the relationship, the management from the human touch. People become combatants for a cause that can never succeed. It is a counterintuitive struggle that turns a "people" strategy into transactions and technology. It only perpetuates the disconnection of two sides that, in reality, are working towards precisely the same goals: selling products and services and caring for the customers who buy them. They work in teams and think they are collaborating on behalf of the customer, but the customer will tell you otherwise.

If collaboration were truly the focus, CRM would become a vehicle to connect all your corporate teams (internal and external partners and channels) with the vision of improving the central relationships of your business through meaningful interactions. CRM would become the first and most foundational step in a series of interconnected strategies that define the relationship and connect to engagement, centricity, service, transparency, and experience strategies. CRM would become the table you gather around to collaborate, improve your understanding of the customer, and become more appreciative of the people that make it happen.

FROM CRM EVOLUTION TO REVOLUTION

There is a lot we know about CRM. To many people CRM means software, so they tend to think of it only in terms of technology. The world has plenty of "CRM" but very little "relationship management." Kudos to the companies that brought us great CRM technology tools and productivity advancements. Kudos to the many talented consultants, experts, gurus, and trainers in this space. CRM software companies have contributed methodologies and best practices to help you implement these tools with ease, on time and on budget. However, more that evolution, CRM needs revolution and a manifesto. A manifesto that commits us to the same goals. Yes, we still need methodologies, and planning guides and technology innovation. But we need a manifesto to help us declare our intentions, motives, and views firmly about CRM and its real application. Manifestos communicate your willingness to accept new ideas and challenge the current status quo leading us away from what CRM really is. Manifestos urge you to set aside preconceived judgments and promote new ideas that enact positive change. Manifestos are about making a stand, and right now, the CRM industry needs one. CRM implementers need it. CRM software companies need it. The people implementing CRM technology need it. Without it, CRM will continue to be a tool for selling and never a tool for building relationships and improving the customer experience.

In the few hours it will take to read this book, I want you to make a commitment to a cause worth fighting. No matter what you do at your company, failure to collaborate to support customers concerns you. Watching it happen should motivate you to change things, regardless of the cost and the sacrifice it takes to make it right. CRM can be the answer, but if it is only about numbers and data, and transactions in a database, then it is not worth doing. It is time to band together to leverage what we have learned in the past fifteen years and use that knowledge to support customer strategies holistically, rather than force technology on people. It is time to speak frankly about our need to collaborate in sharing the idea of customer relationship advocacy and placing its execution in the hands of the people that can progressively affect its outcome.

For years, I have been sharing the following list of "manifesto articles" with my clients at "town hall" style meetings, CRM project launches, and leadership calls. I encourage companies to go through the list together and set the right expectations from the start (before buying software or hiring an implementation partner, if possible). The articles (represented by each section of this book) transcend industry, geography, language, company size, and technology platform. The manifesto "articles" are designed to help your company unite behind a common vision of what CRM accomplishes and how it connects to other customer engagement and service initiatives that result in great customer experiences:

1. CRM must manage ALL the dimensions of the customer relationship: definition, engagement, centricity, service, support, transparency, and experience.

2. CRM is not dead and is far more than just technology. It is also about the strategies that help you build genuine relationships with customers and the people who help them feel rewarded for doing business with you (employees, partners, suppliers, etc.).

3. CRM is a collaborative effort. It requires you eliminate silos across all your business functions.

4. CRM requires transparency. Some of the challenges CRM

unveils can only be solved through honest communication.

5. CRM requires you understand how relationships work; its patterns of establishment, growth, and deterioration.

6. CRM manages the customer and employee interactions that lead to genuine connections. Managing genuine interactions require skill.

7. CRM is about customers. They determine if your CRM efforts are successful, not you.

8. CRM tools are enablers. They help you manage customer relationships with greater efficiency. They do not manage customer relationships for you.

9. CRM is not always out-of-the-box. Understand the investments that make CRM tools work for you.

10. CRM is a journey that will require your commitment and dedication.

I call these a "manifesto" because manifestos kindle the fire of revolution and it is about time for one with CRM. For far too long, CRM initiatives have met an unsightly end because of the emphasis on technology rather than people and the processes that win and retain the right customer, employee, and partner relationships. Revolutionary thinking that compels you to reevaluate CRM's place as a strategy for managing all aspects of the customer relationship may just be the best option. Revolution (from the Latin "revolutio", a turnaround or "revolver" to revolve) is a fundamental change in power or organizational structure.

A manifesto is the tool that unites people in inciting change and sometimes it takes a revolutionary attitude to enact that change. We have to stop saying that CRM is a thing of the past. Instead, we should assert the value of a strategy that so accurately depicts what really keeps us all in business: Customer Relationship Management. It is under that strategy that we will find meaning in customer centricity, engagement, service, and experience initiatives. What is certain is that you must ignite swift and immediate changes to make CRM a success for your company. The CRM industry has to change, in general, to shake off the negative notoriety earned through years of basing CRM strategy and technology on transactions rather than the needs of people (employees and customers alike).

HOW TO BENEFIT FROM THIS BOOK

The book was designed as a tool to promote discussion of the seven articles in the CRM Manifesto with each section representing one of the ten articles:

SECTION 1: SPEAKING ABOUT UNIFICATION

Dives into the seven customer relationship dimensions CRM must manage as a unified customer strategy.

SECTION 2: SPEAKING ABOUT THE ACRONYM

Submits that CRM is exactly that, Customer Relationship Management. In spite of the bad reputation that has marred the acronym, CRM works. This section encourages conversations about what CRM means or will mean for your company and motivates you to focus on collective objectives and goals across the entire business.

SECTION 3: SPEAKING ABOUT COLLABORATION

Calls for each member of your organization to work together to assess customer relationship management initiatives and implement them successfully, together. It encourages conversations about the level of collaboration you will need and the barriers you must overcome to manage ALL aspects of relationship management (including communication, personalization, transparency, and the customer experience itself).

SECTION 4: SPEAKING ABOUT RESOLUTION

Explores the important questions people are asking (or will ask) about CRM and guides you through the best ways to answer them to ensure company-wide support. It encourages transparent, open conversations about the topics people need to understand, and the expectations they need to clarify, in order to engage wholeheartedly.

SECTION 5: SPEAKING ABOUT RELATIONSHIPS

Expands on the similarities between personal and business relationships and expounds on how CRM can be the right strategy to help build them. It encourages conversations about the business relationships you are trying to cultivate and how you are either nurturing them or neglecting them.

SECTION 6: SPEAKING ABOUT INTERACTION

Brings awareness to specific, critical interactions your company must manage for genuine, heartfelt service to result. This section encourages conversations about the particular things we do, or not do, that could make an impact on how you connect to people inside and outside your company.

SECTION 7: SPEAKING ABOUT THE CUSTOMER

Challenges your perceptions of what constitutes CRM success and provides real measurements for ensuring it. This section encourages conversations about the perceptions and measurements you are using to assess the health of your business relationships and align them with customer expectations.

SECTION 8: SPEAKING ABOUT CRM TOOLS

Addresses the role of CRM tools and applications as enablers of the CRM strategy. This section encourages conversations around tool selection and usage, in alignment with the relationship-building processes you have placed at the heart of your business.

SECTION 9: SPEAKING ABOUT INDUSTRY

Offers important considerations for customizing CRM tools to fit the needs of your industry. This section encourages conversations about the level of effort needed to make CRM tools work within your industry and business, and the necessary investments to make it work.

SECTION 10: SPEAKING ABOUT THE JOURNEY

Encourages you to undertake the mandates that can transform your company and the lives of people. It encourages conversations about how to make CRM about more than transactions and metrics and into an effort that impacts the lives of people inside and outside your immediate circles of influence.

The use of the words "encourages" and "conversation" to describe each section is intentional. I wrote the book to   encourage and motivate you to see CRM as a good thing. It encourages you to engage others in conversations that lead to collaboration. Use it before you launch any CRM strategy or engage in discussions about a company-wide CRM effort or technology implementation. Having an understanding of what CRM is, some of the misconceptions about its application, and the central themes of collaboration, relationship building, and critical interactions will give you a better foundation from which to start.

Use it when you need to re-assess your strategy. Businesses change, and with change come the need to reassess the direction of your initiatives. Test your CRM strategy against the precepts of the book to determine if you have consensus and collective support before you take the next step.

Use it when things are not progressing. Remember that this book is about having productive conversations (communication) and collaborations. Lack of a shared vision and unclear expectations can derail any effort. Leverage the conversation and collaboration themes in this book to get everyone moving together, clarify expectations, ask questions within actionable forums that help resolve them, and discuss solutions for succeeding together. While there are a number of compelling books about CRM available to you today, I believe this book is the first focused on encouraging standard and purposeful dialog about CRM across your company in an open collaborative forum.

Zig Ziglar said, "the foundation stones for a balanced success are honesty, character, integrity, faith, love, and loyalty." While we often exclude these ideas from business conversations, and while some of you may find them uncomfortable to express at work, they are, nonetheless, a big part of this book. I talk about being loyal and accountable to customers and about showing sincere love for the people who care about them. I talk about having faith in people, and I encourage you to assess with character and integrity the reasons why you do what you do. That's because without a foundation of accountability, integrity, and trust none of what we do in sales, marketing or support matters in the end.

PART ONE

SECTION 1

SPEAKING ABOUT UNIFICATION

CRM MUST MANAGE ALL THE DIMENSIONS OF THE CUSTOMER RELATIONSHIP.

(DEFINITION, ENGAGEMENT, CENTRICITY, SERVICE, SUPPORT, TRANSPARENCY, AND EXPERIENCE)

uni·fy \ verb \ˈyü-nə-ˌfī\ : to cause (people
or things) to be brought together.[2]

**"I mean, the great secret is that an orchestra can
actually play without a conductor at all. Of course,
a great conductor will have a concept and will help
them play together and unify them."**

- DJoshua Bell, Violinist

I will begin by saying unapologetically that this book is about CRM (Customer Relationship Management). It supports the strategies and technology that manage relationships with customers, but also employees and partners. It defends the use of the acronym some have grown to distrust (although for the wrong reason, as I will explain in detail later). It argues the need for CRM's place in business as a fundamental strategy for business growth. It rallies for the validation of "CRM" as the practices, processes, and strategies we use to win and keep the right customers. It emphasizes the need to support all the people who care for the customer as part of a unified strategy that eliminates silos and improves collaboration.

This book doesn't try to convince you to use words like "experience," "engagement," or "centricity" to replace the CRM acronym as a way to apologize for getting it wrong for so many years. Instead, you will learn that the methodologies embedded so soundly in customer relationship management are valid and mature. They are more relevant than ever in light of the disruptions created by new technology and changes in culture. You will read that CRM has been, in fact, the right strategy all along. That our evolving understanding of the way customer experience measures customer defection does not replace CRM, but encourages closer attention to its impact on Customer Experience Index and Net Promoter Score analysis.

Changes in technology and new research in customer behavior influenced the revision of this book in particular, mainly because as this revision was written, the customer service industry experienced (and continues to experience) a personality crisis. Companies cling desperately to terms preceded by the word "customer" and crown them THE reigning strategy to follow without a clear understanding of how this will affect ongoing strategies. Technology vendors and consulting firms, eager to cash in on trends, aggravate the situation by marketing to the hype, encouraging the use of tools that are good remedies for some of the symptoms; not the cure to an illness companies have suffered for years. The illness is our departure from the practices that build genuine relationships with the people who allow us to build and grow our businesses: customers, employees, and business partners.

Let me emphasize that this book does not discount that many companies are using CRM tools successfully to sell and market their products and provide exceptional service to customers. Or that many companies understand that CRM is the strategy we use to define how we win and keep customers (regardless of technology tools). Neither does it ignore the leadership of authors and thought leaders in customer engagement, experience, centricity, and service. On the contrary, it contends that years of failed implementations and strategy investment directed at winning and keeping customers have forced us to abandon the practices that did not work, compelled by smarter customers that demand change. The "proven" methods have finally risen to the top. We have a second chance to leverage what we have learned and execute a more collaborative and unified approach to managing business relationships; an approach for which CRM can be the foundation.

Understanding where CRM fits within a unified customer strategy is essential to its success, as is your understanding of the strategies that CRM supports.

A UNIFIED CUSTOMER STRATEGY

I want you to put this book aside for a moment and participate in a little exercise with me. I want you to detach your thinking from the "customer relationship" and "employee relationship" or "partner relationship" aspects of this book, even if you are reading it at work. I want you to take your mind away from what you do for a living and concentrate on your personal relationships instead, for a moment. Think of a person or persons in your personal life with whom you spend a lot of your time.

On a blank sheet of paper, I want you to write down the first thought or reaction that comes to mind when you read the following words:

Expectations

Engagement

Personal attention

Service...

Support

Transparency

Experience

Write each word down, and then take the time to (in as much detail as possible) express what each word means to you in relation to this person. In case you are having difficulty with this drill, let me go through each word as it applies to the people with whom I spend most of my personal time:

EXPECTATION

My relationship with my five children is very important to me. To see a genuine relationship evolve between us is a priority for me. I know that my role as a dad defines the expectations and responsibilities of the relationship. The way we talk to, behave toward, and deal with one another is defined by the roles and responsibilities of the parent-child relationship. As a parent, my kids expect me to make an investment of time and money that facilitates a safe environment for them to grow. As a father, I expect them to listen and follow my guidance until they are adults. I expect them to honor their mom and respect adults and contribute to society. As my children, they expect me to care for them. Understanding the expectations, risks, investments, and rewards involved in being a parent helps me become a better one. When there is an imbalance (anytime either party sees that the risks are too high or the rewards too low during an interaction), we experience a deterioration in the relationship. When the kids feel that what I do to build the relationship is rewarding, the relationship solidifies, and the bond strengthens. When I do things that put my time, commitments, and investment in them at risk the relationship deteriorates. Building a relationship with my kids is challenging at times, but it brings great joy to my life.

Similarly, I understand the responsibilities required of me as a spouse. The spouse-relationship also defines the responsibilities of the role. When I think of the word "expectation," I think of the investment, responsibilities, boundaries, risks, rewards, and commitments it takes to make that relationship work. I make greater investments in my parent-relationship than my neighbor-relationship because of the greater significance of my parent relationship.

ENGAGEMENT

While there are aspects of my role as a parent that apply equally and (most of the time) fairly to all my kids, they are as different from one another as any five children could be. My oldest daughter wanted to be a mom more than anything in the world (and is a great mom today). Her brothers developed individual interests in language and philosophy, music, and athletics respectively. Our youngest daughter is still trying to figure it out, but we have some ideas about her intentions to rule the world. I affectionately refer to them as the mom, the philosopher, the musician, the athlete, and the princess. What worked for one child in terms of motivation and interest did not always work for the next. To "engage" with my children I had to get creative. That's because effective "engagement" requires that you induce participation and interlock someone's attention. Even their preferred methods of communicating range anywhere from a text to a long focused conversation at the dinner table. I will let you guess which son (the philosopher, the musician, or the athlete) preferred the face-to-face in-depth analysis of the emotional benefits of staying up past bedtime.

Engagement is participative (involves participation); something parents struggle to get from kids sometimes. Not just from the little ones, but teenagers have a hard time committing to interactions that are engaging and to communications that are meaningful. When they do, the channel(s) they prefer to use to communicate and the attention span they are willing to commit to the conversation differs based on their interest, goals, age, and even where they rank amongst their siblings. When I think of the word "engagement," I think of the best ways to communicate with my kids and hold their attention and participation.

PERSONAL ATTENTION

When you focus your attention on someone you are exercising centricity. Part of the investment I spoke about earlier requires that I regularly focus on the specific needs of each child. Centricity is that unique and individual need at the center of their life. The medical term "centric" is a great way to explain it since it means "relating to a nerve center". Getting to the nerve center of someone's need is a big part of building relationships. When I think of the word "centric," I think of the individual needs of each child. I think about actionable steps to listen and gain their engagement so I can personalize the response and the steps to help meet those needs.

SERVICE AND SUPPORT

In spite of how tightly intertwined the ideas of service and support are, there is an important difference between the two. Service is proactive, and support is reactive. Yes, service can be any act that benefits another person, especially when there is no tangible benefit to you. However, the word service also defines the set of responsibilities attached to a role. For example, as a parent, I am responsible for taking physical, emotional, and spiritual care of my children. Those responsibilities are defined by the role and largely by our culture. In the United States, until they are eighteen years old, I am legally responsible for what my kids do. I am bound by law to supply food and shelter for them. After they are of age, I no longer have a responsibility to provide for them. However, there are times when they need me and I respond with wholehearted support. I have a connection to my kids that goes beyond parental "responsibility." It is my sense of "accountability" that compels me to support them. I do not have to provide financially when they are in college. That is no longer my "responsibility," but I do because I support them and their aspirations.

The transition between service and support (what we "have" to do and what we "want" to do... or even what is "right" to do) is seamless for most parents. I do not stop to rationalize when I am serving and supporting my family, or anyone else with whom I have a close relationship. However, seeing that there is a difference reminds me to adjust my attitude.

TRANSPARENCY

When I make my intentions, expectations, engagements, interactions, and communications transparent, I build trust with my kids. Transparency builds trust because it allows people visibility and accessibility into your intentions. It shows people that what you say or do is free from pretense or deceit. My goal is for my kids, spouse, friends, and business associates to trust me. Therefore, I aim to be as transparent as possible with my words and actions. I could never achieve trust without transparency. With kids, transparency requires a lot of courage because kids love to take control of situations where their "opponent" (that would be you) shows all their cards. Transparency shows kids that you are serious and willing to take a risk in order to accomplish something. It also has an impact on you, as it motivates you to be consistent and honest; connecting all your interactions consistently regardless of the method you use to communicate. When I think of the word "transparency," I think of infusing trust into my words and actions as I interact with my children.

EXPERIENCE

I hope that as my children become adults and parents themselves (one already is) that they will have joyful memories of our experiences as a family. The word experience represents both the time we spend observing or participating in something, and the collection of those individual moments. The experience of living is composed of many individual experiences. Good experiences bond relationships and cause people to share that feeling of unity with others. Therefore, in relationship to my kids, the experience is each moment, and the collection of moments, we get to spend together and the emotional connection and memories that result from those moments.

When I spend time with my children (together and individually), I always ask them: "are you getting what you need from me?", "Am I making it easy to interact and communicate (especially during the teenage years)?" When the answer is "yes" to both questions, I know I am creating an emotional connection between us that will make it easier to go through the not-so-great experiences. Asking the "experience" questions helps me evaluate the health of the relationship.

BACK TO WORK THINGS

Switching your attention back to your business life, I want you to complete this exercise again. Take a break if you need to. Call the person you were just thinking about if you want. When you are ready, on a new sheet of paper I want you to write down the first thought that comes to mind when you read the same seven words: Expectations, Engagement, Centricity, Service, Support, Transparency, and Experience. This time, however, I don't want you to think about a personal relationship. I want you instead to think about your customers. Choose a customer with whom you do business regularly. If your main customers are individual consumers, I want you to think about your regulars. If your primary customers or clients are companies, I want you to think of both the company and the people with whom you do business regularly. I will give you a moment...

Most of the people that complete this exercise share that it was far more difficult to complete it while thinking about customers. They also tell me that they had difficulty connecting each of the words to the same customer or company. Why is it so difficult to see business relationships as "relationships" that have similar patterns of growth and deterioration as those we experience in personal relationships? After all, many of you spend more time interacting with customers than your family members and friends. How can "customer relationship management" be about skillfully growing your customer relationships when you only address one dimension of it or are confused about how relationship building even works? Perhaps most relevant to the topic of this book is, why do we continue to see CRM as a sales database rather than a strategy for investing in the right relationships, engaging customers based on their most central needs, and focusing on service and transparency that usher great customer experiences? These are all terms you already hear at work every day: relationship, engagement, centricity, service, support, transparency, and experience. Why, then, are companies not seeing the connection between them?

As with personal relationships, customer relationships follow patterns. They have many dimensions. More specifically, they require establishment and growth in these seven, very distinct but interconnected areas. An orchestrated approach to CRM that manages each dimension of the customer relationship is imperative; especially for companies seeking to eliminate functional and organizational silos. Your company may already have a customer relationship strategy in place, CRM tools to support it, digital customer engagement assets to implement omnichannel communications, service and support agreements (SLAs) and customer experience and NPS (Net Promoter Score) analytics to evaluate customer economics. But if you do not view customer relationship, engagement, centricity, service, support, transparency, and experience as joined parts of the same strategy, then you are not managing the customer relationship. You are too busy managing disconnected aspects of interacting with customers, not building a relationship with them.

Only a unified approach can result in effective customer relationship management strategies and technology adoption. It is a dangerous component to overlook because companies must have a clear view of customer relationships and customer segments in whom to invest to deliver on their value proposition. When companies fail to see the customer relationship holistically they also fail to see their business holistically. A unified customer strategy that puts the customer at the center of the business and builds relationships from the customer's perspective will help you invest in the right activities, using the right resources and partnerships, through the right channels. It will improve how you evaluate your cost structure and open new revenue streams.

An effective implementation of CRM (strategy and technology) goes beyond the 360-degree view of customer information and interactions. CRM is the strategy that gives you real-time insight into the health of the seven dimensions that constitute the customer relationship. It uses insight from each component of the relationship, which you can use to educate the business and help you adjust investment in key activities, key resources, key partnerships, channels, cost structure and value proposition.

To understand the customer you have to understand each of the components that, together, help you win and keep them. This relationship-building approach is also applicable to employee and business partner relationships, but let's focus on the customer for now:

CUSTOMER RELATIONSHIP

CRM manages relationship definition, expectations, and commitment. Customer Relationship strategies help you define the right customer segments to whom you will effectively deliver your value proposition. Customer relationship strategies and tools help you identify the right people and companies to whom you can deliver value. Customers continually evaluate your ability to meet and support that commitment. If you do, they will subsequently recommend you to others. The longevity of the commitment will depend on how customers perceive the value of doing business with you. They are constantly assessing the balance of risks and rewards and, when the scale tips against you, they will leave. Placing the word "customer" as a prefix to the word "relationship" creates immediate expectations and commitments.

Understanding the expectations, risks, investments, and rewards customers expect is the foundation for building relationships. You also have to evaluate if the risks and investments you make on certain customers is too high.

CUSTOMER ENGAGEMENT

CRM manages level of engagement. For "engagement" to be true to its definition it must induce participation and interlock someone's attention. Otherwise, it is not engagement at all. Companies tend to use the term "customer engagement" mistakenly as an umbrella for "all things customer." Engagement is participative, and that word does not describe the behavior we experience from many customers. Customer engagement must be participative and (and I am not flippant here) "engaging." Perhaps one of the most understated aspects of customer engagement is that the word engagement itself suggests "interest." Walker's "Customers 2020: The Future of B-to-B Customer Experience" defines engagement as a tailored metric consisting of four elements:

- Product Usage - the breadth and depth of product penetration (e.g., purchase patterns, product usage metrics, etc.)

- Sentiment - the frequency and magnitude of customer thoughts and feelings (e.g., NPS, customer loyalty, sentiment on social media, etc.)

- Involvement - the ways in which customers interact with the business (e.g., do customers attend events, are they willing to be a reference, will they share a case study, do they engage via social media, do they co-create, etc.)

- Competitive Status - how engaged is the customer with the competition (e.g., share of wallet)

What I appreciate most about the metrics Walker identifies, is that they measure important aspects of true engagement, such as:

- Attracting and holding a customer's interest

- Customer Involvement

- Holding the customer's attention

- Inducing customer participation

- Forging mutual agreements

Just as important as the result of "engaging" are the channels you use to accomplish that. The term "customer engagement channels" must describe conduits to and from the customer, which lead to effective engagement.

CUSTOMER CENTRICITY

CRM manages specific needs. This term (also used a lot to describe customer strategies in general) is actually more about the personalized attention you give customers. It is what a customer needs to feel you are paying attention to their particular needs. Centricity and Experience are closely connected because it could take personalization to make a customer feel that you are addressing their needs, making it easy for them and connecting them emotionally to your brand (the three components that measure customer experience). Personalizing the experience to the individual or company and their need facilitates engagement. It makes customers feel that you are making an investment in the relationship.

Often overlooked is that Customer Centricity includes the processes and guidelines you implement to ensure everyone makes the customer the center of your business. When you say that something is "centric," you define it as being located in the center. You direct everything towards it. Everything is built around it and in relationship to it. A customer-centric company makes the customer the most important or pivotal relationship of their business.

CUSTOMER SERVICE AND SUPPORT

CRM manages how you are being responsive and accountable to customers. Customer Service and Support strategies are designed to show a genuine commitment to customers. They are part of how you make engagements "engaging," and how you make customers feel rewarded for doing business with you. I intentionally separate the terms "service" and "support" because customers perceive them differently. Service is proactive because you have a responsibility to provide customers with the service you promised them when they purchased your products or service. Service is a guarantee you made which says that, should your product fail to perform as promised, you will do whatever is reasonable to fix or replace it. Service also includes the terms under which you will do that. There is, however, a "reactive" choice you make when there are no service level agreements (SLA's) or a responsibility to give the customer what they are asking. It is the behavior and attitude that shows customers you are willing to go the "extra mile" to address unforeseen needs. Service is your responsibility, but support shows accountability to making the customer the center of your business. Using the term "service" is sufficient as long as you recognize that service is an act of responsibility AND accountability. However, CRM must manage both. It does not always produce a tangible commodity other than an exceptional experience for customers, but, after all, that is exactly what keeps them your customer.

Some companies see service and support roles as separate functions (such as customer service versus technical support). Both functions require an attitude of responsibility and accountability. So does our attitude towards the customer, in general, regardless of your role.

CUSTOMER TRANSPARENCY

CRM manages how you build trust with customers. When you make your intentions, expectations, engagements, interactions and communications transparent, you build trust. Transparency builds trust because it allows customers visibility and accessibility into your intentions. Not only transparent about what your brand is and does but about how you prove that it is free from pretense or deceit. Transparency builds customer trust because people need visibility and accessibility into your intentions before they make a decision to buy and continue to buy from you. Trust in your ability to deliver on your promise also motivates customers to recommend you to others. Transparency infuses trust into your words and actions as you interact with your customers.

When I speak to my readers about transparency, some hesitate with concerns about too much transparency diminishing competitive advantage. I respond with this excerpt from an online Fortune

Magazine article by John Hagel III and John Seely Brown (April 2, 2014) entitled "How to deepen customer loyalty: Be transparent."

"In 2008, Domino's Pizza (now Domino's) took to the Internet to survey its customers. The customers made their feelings clear: they didn't love the crust, the sauce, or the cheese. Perhaps nothing new in a customer survey, but then Domino's took the unusual step of opening up further — actually sharing the survey results publicly and asking customers to help fix the problems. In 18 months, the company received thousands of messages through social media; it invited regular customers to try its pizzas and made changes along the way, even while it lost some customers. When the company re-launched its product at the end of 2009 with a series of commercials featuring its troubles and solutions, customer response was largely positive. And rather than a one-time experiment, Domino's continued the relationship and now has more than 9 million fans on Facebook and 483 thousand followers on Twitter. The company's stock rose to $72.18 in February 2014 from $7.73 in 2009."

Customer Transparency is more than a marketing tactic. It is good business.

CUSTOMER EXPERIENCE

CRM manages customer economics. Customer Experience strategies represent the sum of your interactions with customers. It is a term that is getting a lot of attention these days because it accurately describes the way customers decide to do business with you, depending on how you deliver functionality, accessibility, and connection. Good experiences bond relationships and compel customers to share that feeling of connection to your brand with others. When I interact with customers, I always ask them if they are getting what they need from me and if I make it easy for them to interact with my company and with me. When the answer is "yes" to both questions, I know I am creating an emotional connection that will keep them my customer. We will discuss Customer Experience at length throughout the book and explain the importance of incorporating Cx metrics and activity into the CRM effort.

CRM AND THE UNIFIED CUSTOMER STRATEGY

What surprises me most about how people react to these seven words is that they are all embedded deeply in our business vocabulary. We already use them to describe parts of our customer efforts. We build our companies on the needs of customers, with whom we establish business relationships. We engage them through a number of channels that may require a more customer-centric approach (retailers know this very well). Customers expect exceptional service and support. The average customer wants a transparent experience with your brand, regardless of the store, mobile app, or website where they buy your products. However, when you try to connect each of the efforts, resources, and technology that represent each of these concepts, people struggle to connect and collaborate.

If I told you that in my household we assign the responsibility for defining relationship, engagement, and experience to different family members, without feedback or collaboration from one another, you would be correct to call this a "dysfunctional family." You know that relationship building can't be an isolated strategy. You know that each of these seven aspects support the same relationship. Why, then, do companies think they can make that same mistake with customer relationships without immense impact to their business and without creating silos? Why are sales and marketing organizations responsible for defining the customer relationship while contact centers define (through obsolete metrics) the way your company engages customers? Why is customer experience a separate function that sometimes does not even fall under sales, marketing, or support (much less lead the people who are actually talking to customers)? Why is customer centricity something we insist on addressing primarily through technology? Why is IT left to solve so many of the problems that help build customer relationships? Why do we continue to build dysfunctional customer strategies thinking this will ever work?

HAVING THE RIGHT CONVERSATIONS

I believe that communication and collaboration enable successful customer relationship management implementations. To build meaningful and profitable relationships with customers you have to talk about what that relationship needs to thrive. Then you have to be willing to speak frankly about the things preventing you from working together to manage customer relationships. I know that the business focus has shifted to "customer experience" and that it seems a bit outdated to emphasize the importance of CRM. However, customer experience, while essential to how we measure the quality of our customer relationships, is only one of seven components needed to implement a holistic customer relationship management strategy successfully. CRM is the strategy that manages the seven dimensions of the customer relationship, including the level of investment in the relationship itself. Managing the seven strategies as parts of a Unified Customer Strategy, using CRM as a foundation, eliminates silos and increases collaboration while being inclusive of customer experience practices. Regardless of how you feel about CRM strategies, practices or tools, it is still the best first step in working together for the good of the customer, and the employees and partners who serve them.

Speaking frankly about the seven unified customer strategies themselves is the first conversation you should have with your company. You have to understand what CRM is actually managing (expectations, engagement, centricity, service, support, transparency, and experience) before you do anything else. Then use the following sections of the book to facilitate honest conversations that will lead to a clear vision of CRM implementation and practice that manages the customer relationship holistically.

SECTION 2

SPEAKING ABOUT THE ACRONYM

CRM IS NOT DEAD AND IS FAR
MORE THAN TECHNOLOGY.

ac·ro·nym \ noun \'a-krə-ˌnim\: a word
formed from the initial letter or letters of
each of the successive parts or major parts
of a compound term[3]

"A lost person or article is still what it is, still valuable in itself, but in the wrong place, disconnected from its purpose and unable to be or do whatever it is intended to be or do."

- David Winter, *What's in a Word*

You have probably read a number of definitions for the term "customer relationship management" or CRM:

"Customer relationship management (CRM) is a widely-implemented model for managing a company's interactions with customers and prospects. It involves using technology to organize, automate, and synchronize business processes—principally sales activities, but also those for marketing, customer service, and technical support." - Dr. Robert Shaw's book, "Computer Aided Marketing & Selling" (1991).

"The overall goals are to find, attract, and win new clients, service and retain those the company already has, entice former clients to return, and reduce the costs of marketing and client service." 2009 Gartner Inc. article entitled "What's 'Hot' in CRM Applications in 2009" by Ed Thompson.

"Customer relationship management describes a company-wide business strategy including customer interface departments as well as other departments." - DestinationCRM.com

While viewed from different stages of CRM technology and practice, these definitions agree on one very important point: CRM is about managing your interactions with customers. In spite of the changes to the companies selling CRM software and consulting services, the purpose of CRM has never changed. Over the years, companies have used different methods for maintaining customer information (from the paper file folders to the 360 degree-based technology we use now). But the ideas that customers are the lifeblood of your businesses, that you need a strategy for establishing the correct relationships with them, and that you must be intentional about how you manage your interactions remain consistent.

THE ACRONYM ISN'T THE ISSUE

The use of the CRM acronym is under great scrutiny. After a long debate about the use of the word "contact" for a strategy that manages customer relationships, we began a campaign that resulted in the use of "customer relationship management" as the preferred label of the industry. Then comes trouble in the form of highly publicized reports about CRM high failure rates.

Studies conducted by reputable companies like Gartner, AMR, and Forester, in collaboration with companies using the technology, published reports stating that between 2001 and 2009 as many as 50 percent of CRM implementations were viewed as failures from the customer's point of view when asked the question "Did it meet expectations?"

As a result, CRM software vendors started to lobby for new terms to replace the term CRM for terms like "xRM." Likewise, customers began to use alternate terms to prevent internal decision-makers from eliminating their CRM initiatives over rumors of difficult implementations, poor usability, and fragmented strategies supported by software solutions that presented serious privacy and data security concerns.

The idea of retiring the term CRM is alive, fueled by groups that want to replace it with the term "Customer Experience Management" (Cx for short). This mistake not only misses the definition of what CRM is but also undermines that customer experience is an important part of what CRM enables. Here is why:

1. Customer Experience is a term that refers to the interactions a customer has with you, your employees, and your vendors over the life of the relationship.

2. A healthy customer relationship relies on the customer evaluating each experience individually and collectively against other experiences with your brand.

3. Relationships are the affiliations, associations, and connections we have or want to have with customers. A relationship is what we so eagerly aim to establish with the people that keep us in business. This includes companies that sell to customers only once because, regardless of the number of times they sell to someone, they still have to build a strategy to identify who their best customers are.

4. Therefore, customer experiences are what customers use to determine if they want that relationship to grow or end.

There are many terms used interchangeably to define a company's goal of building relationships that lead to mutual benefit. There are also terms like Customer Experience Management (CEM) that dive further into the channels customers use to building and strengthen those relationships. But neither Cx or CEM replace what CRM does. They are interconnected, supportive strategies we use to win and retain customers.

MANY STRATEGIES, ONE FOCUS: THE CUSTOMER

All you have to do is attend a company-wide meeting or conference call to realize that there are many disconnected customer efforts underway at your company. Perhaps out of urgency or simply as a result of poor communication, people are involved in efforts that should compliment one another but instead, get in the way of one another. And not just disconnected from CRM, but disconnected from all the efforts you make to win, keep, or regain the customer. While one side of your company works on centralizing access to customer information, another works on the communication channels your customers use to reach you while yet another creates metrics around the customer experience. Unfortunately, these organizations often work in silos, never collaborating in their efforts to win the customer, although all along sharing that vision.

Psychologist Abraham Maslow is credited with saying, "I suppose it is tempting, if the only tool you have is a hammer, to treat everything as if it were a nail." Such is the temptation for organizations to focus on what they know, and overlook what is happening elsewhere in the company. The truth is that there are many well-intended people in your company doing the right things. They are simply not working together to understand the planets in the customer strategies universe, all of which revolve around the customer.

Here is what a Unified Customer Strategy looks like:

1. A unified approach to Customer Strategies helps you invest in the right resources, methods, and technology. It helps you assess the health of your business strategies, such as your value proposition to customer segments, the channels you use to sell your products and services, the finances that fund it, and the key resources, activities, and partnerships that keep your business running. It allows sales, marketing, and support organizations to support your customers and the needs of the business in unison.

2. First, Customer Relationship Strategies help you determine the right customers for your business so you can truly invest and care for them.

3. Then, Customer Engagement Strategies help define the best ways to connect with customers through channels that facilitate clear communication. It is like building a bridge that lets customers get to you from where they are, and you to

where they are.

4. With a strong customer engagement foundation, you can make each interaction intentional and Customer-Centric. Remember, people want you to treat them as if they are your only customer.

5. You can now develop Customer Service strategies that define the level of service you can and will provide to customers.

6. All of this delivered in a way that is transparent to the customer. All they see is a single company brand dedicated to a seamless experience for everyone.

7. From here, Customer Experience strategies monitor and ensure that customers are able to accomplish what they needed when they came to you to begin with so you can maintain positive, memorable experiences that motivate customers to buy and recommend you to others.

These are the strategies that work together to make the customer feel rewarded for doing business with you.

IT'S ABOUT EXPECTATIONS

Where, then, is the disconnect regarding the continued role of CRM as a (very much alive) customer strategy? It is in forgetting that the studies that instilled such lack of confidence in CRM did not debate the use of the acronym or its definition, and most certainly not its value. Rather, they asked (frankly), "did it meet expectations?" It was of the responses to that question (did it meet expectation?) that the negative sentiment began. While a great number of CRM projects meet deadlines and launch successfully, those responsible for rating its success do not think it meets expectations.

The misuse of terms and studies, and the rhetoric of so-called gurus about what CRM is and is not, have made CRM unrecognizable from its original self and disconnected from its purpose, unable to function as intended. Rather than do away with the acronym or replace it with something else, we have a responsibility to address the expectation problem. We must answer that question honestly. Did CRM fail or have we been trying to meet the wrong expectations all along? CRM has always been a vehicle to connect all the people in your company with the vision of improving the central relationships of your business through meaningful interactions.

To overlook that CRM is one of seven components in the unified customer strategies is perhaps the greatest contributor to CRM misperception and failure. We rely on CRM as the solution to our customer visibility problems but overlook that relationship management has many facets and dimensions that you have relinquished to other organizations within your company. Those organizations then manage the customer relationship from their perspective, not connecting the pieces. The correct expectation of what CRM is (and what it does) is that it is both the first step in the process of building customer relationships and the strategy that connects all the other customer strategies to one another. CRM is the foundation that helps establish the relationship and helps you execute on your goals for maintaining it through engagement, centricity, service, support, transparency, and experiences that make you and the customer feel there is value in the relationship. It all comes full circle. When you start saying that customer experience trumps customer relationship management because CRM is outdated, or that customer experience replaces it, then you are out of touch with how to build customer relationships.

The acronym is just a flag under which we march to accomplish this purpose. Call your customer program whatever you want, as long as you connect how experience and relationship work together. Being all "hung up" on the acronym will only distract you. After all, more than one hundred and twenty acronyms use the letters "CRM." Tied for number one are "customer relationship management" and "crew resource management." That does not change what CRM should be or that it must be about managing relationships holistically as we have discussed.

IT TAKES A VILLAGE

Focusing on labels also has the adverse effect of taking the attention away from the people who contribute to the customer-centric CRM effort. CRM is not just a strategy to address the needs of the customer, but also the needs of all the people that help you serve them.

The customer relationship effort is the responsibility of the entire body of people working together to serve the customer. A "corporation" from the Latin word "corpus" or "body" is a group of people united or regarded as united in one body. The idea of "customer relationship" management helps us keep the focus on the people at the heart of our effort, the customer. The idea of a body of people working together acknowledges that CRM is a strategy that aims to identify and group the whole body of people collaborating to serve the customer. We cannot ignore the people who collectively help win and keep them.

In CRM, the relationship that exists between the members of the "corpus" and their relationship to the customer impact your ability to identify leads, manage sales processes, sell product, and deliver quality customer service. Everyone in the company manages the customer experiences CRM supports. The shift to the mindset of the various corporate relationship entities managing the customer experience allows you to build strategies that reveal new insight into how to serve them best. CRM is not just about the interaction of one person with the customer, it is about the interactions of the "corpus" with the customer and each other. Often overlooked are these important internal conversations.

CRM helps create a clearer picture of how customers behave, engage you, and respond to the way you treat them. An "isolated" conversation with a call center agent, viewed side-by-side with other previously "isolated" interactions may reveal proactive ways to improve that customer's experience and make your business processes more adaptive. It sometimes feels like sales, marketing, and support organizations create completely different roads for the customer to travel (roads that lead to where THEY want customers to go). When we tackle CRM together, we stop trying to force customers to travel our independent path, and we become part of THEIR journey, together; a journey (no longer "linear") that starts and ends where THEY want it to. Customers are not confined by how you want them to buy. It is not a guided tour through a location, controlled by you as the guide. It is controlled by the customer who wants a "theme park" experience; choosing the attractions they want to ride when they want to ride them, but having a good experience regardless of where they start the adventure (for each ride and the theme park as a whole).

THE V-GER EFFECT

This advice to collaborate and contribute information about customer behavior comes with a warning. CRM is indeed a great source for maintaining accurate information about the customer. Unfortunately, some companies err in the use of CRM tools as a repository of ALL data without a strategy for making it useful. It is a lot like the central theme of the first Star Trek movie (Star

Trek the Motion Picture, 1979). To provide some context to you who did not see the movie... The crew of the Starship Enterprise encounters a spacecraft so massive that, in its journey towards earth, leaves destruction in its path. As Kirk and the crew find themselves at the center of the craft, we learn that (spoiler alert) this is, in fact, the 20th-century Earth space probe Voyager-6.

Somewhere along its journey to collect Information, an alien race modified its original mission by mistakenly thinking this vessel was designed to learn "all that could be learned." As a result, the vessel, now named "Vger," grew beyond manageable measures and became destructive in its journey to fulfill its true purpose.

Some CRM strategies and tools are a lot like that. The original goal of a strategy for collecting meaningful information for assessing and building customer relationships becomes a destructive effort to collect customer data beyond reasonable expectations. Curiously, some companies even change the name of their CRM systems. Some do so to help people adopt CRM by aligning it with the company culture. However, a number of companies do so to turn CRM into a massive repository of data that, over time, becomes unmanageable.

The idea of using CRM to manage customer marketing, acquisition, and retention information across departments is within CRM's scope. So is the idea of buying mailing lists and leveraging the power of CRM tools to identify strong prospects and clean up data. However, CRM becomes unmanageable when it becomes all things to all people; an unkempt and outdated Rolodex of customers, vendors, and anyone else with a name and address. When you use CRM that way, you reduce the effectiveness of the business processes it is designed to manage.

CONNECTING CRM WITH BUSINESS NEEDS

One of the most frequent questions I hear people ask at trade shows and business conferences where I speak is "how do I connect CRM to our business goals?" The second most frequent question is "how do I get the budget to invest in CRM and other customer strategies and tools?" It is frustrating to read a book like this one only to return to the reality of no budget to fund and support your goals. It feels like a "catch 22" to create a strategy that addresses both issues: Connecting CRM to your company's business strategy AND getting CRM funded. As I mention earlier, you may also have to contend with the negative connotation CRM carries, making it harder for your finance team to invest. The truth is that just as the past failure of CRM is associated with having the wrong expectations of its function, companies also have wrong expectations about its business impact.

In 2010, Alexander Osterwalder and Yves Pigneur, supported by 470 business practitioners, wrote the book "Business Model Generation." It is a handbook for visionaries, game changers, challengers, and anyone modeling new and existing businesses.

It is a fantastic guide that gives companies insight into the nature of business. It is also a great instrument for designing business processes for CRM through the development of a "business model canvas" (a tool for describing, analyzing, and designing business models).

What makes Business Model Generation so applicable to CRM is that no CRM strategy can succeed without an honest view of how CRM business processes support the foundational building blocks of every business:

- Customer Segments

- Value Proposition

- Channels

- Customer Relationships

- Revenue Stream

- Key Resources

- Key Activities

- Key Partnerships

- Cost Structure

Throughout the book, the authors stop to ask penetrating questions about how a business creates, delivers, and captures value. By asking business stakeholders to ask questions and describe, through the nine building blocks, how a company intends to make money, the canvas helps you focus on the most critical aspects of your business.

Customer relationship management is identified as one of the nine blocks and defined as the strategies and methods by which "customer relationships are established and maintained with each customer segment." Note that the definition does not separate CRM as an independent part of building a business, but as relational to the other building blocks that make up our business.

It is not surprising that there is such a disconnect among business stakeholders about CRM when they see CRM as belonging only to sales, marketing, or support functions. It is also not surprising that customer relationship and customer experience efforts struggle to get C-level buy-in and sponsorship when they are unable to connect its value and support to the other parts of the business.

Here is a list of the nine building blocks used in "The Business Model Canvas" and the essential alignment you must make to CRM.

CUSTOMER SEGMENTS:

By far my most favorite quote about customers comes from Dr. Michael LeBoeuf, who said, "Every company's greatest assets are its customers because without customers there is no company."

The most fundamental question a business must ask is, "who is my customer?" CRM allows us to answer questions about the people for whom you create value. It also allows you to identify which ones should or should not be your customer based on the level of investment you make to win and keep them. CRM allows you to divide customers into the segments your business will support and group them based on attributes, such as common needs and behaviors.

Your company should ask questions such as "how should we use CRM to efficiently segment our customers" and "how do we organize our customer to validate and support our offerings and identify the types of channels and relationships we will need to support them?" If your CRM strategy does not address the question "for whom are you creating value?" you have missed the most important first step in your CRM approach and what you should be communicating to your business leadership.

VALUE PROPOSITION:

With a clear understanding of "who" the customer is, we can identify the value we deliver to them. CRM strategies often account for the products and services you will include in a CRM system and use for sales and opportunity management, quote, orders, and invoices. CRM, as a strategy, must also answer the questions of "which one of your customer's problems are you helping to solve?" and "what products and services are you offering to each customer segment?"

These questions are more about which customer needs you are satisfying than about what specific products and services you are importing into your CRM system. Accounting for the value a service or product offers each customer segment allows you to determine price and usability. If you cannot associate value yield with the products and services you are offering to the customer, by customer segment, you may not be meeting your customer's needs.

CHANNELS:

Just as important as identifying value proposition, is the vehicle you will use to deliver that value to customers. In an evolving customer economy like ours, those "channels" are not only defined by you but also by how customers want to be reached. Channels are the important customer touch points where they make decisions about your value. Your CRM strategy must plan for expedient ways to report who you are reaching via those channels, which channels work best and why, and how they are integrated with customer routines.

Channels are where customers create an impression of you and how much you care about meeting their needs. If your CRM strategy does not identify the channels your customer uses and needs, and where and when meaningful interactions happen, you won't be able to create processes that work for your business and the customer.

CUSTOMER RELATIONSHIP:

The intentional marriage of the terms "customer" and "relationship" helps us define the purpose of establishing the relationship to begin with. Just as the term "family relationship" establishes boundaries for the types of interactions that are encouraged or discouraged, so does the term "customer relationship." Within the customer relationship framework, we aim to establish relationships with people we want to win or keep as customers. This immediately allows us to determine who fits within our CRM strategy.

However, customer relationship also requires us to ask, "What types of relationships do each of our Customer Segments expect us to establish and maintain with them?" This expectation requires thought and planning in order to deliver correctly. If your CRM strategy is not evaluating the current ways you are establishing and maintaining your customer relationships, how these processes are integrated with the rest of your business model, and how much it costs you, you may be investing in the wrong customer relationships.

REVENUE STREAM:

Remember when the now popular single-cup serve coffee brewers became popular to buy? At the time, it was well within the norm to pay more than $50 per pound of coffee to use it. To many people, pods and K-Cups, which are sold in much smaller quantities, appear to have a lower cost per cup because you are only making as much coffee as you will drink. But when you compare the cost to when the cups first became available (Nespresso Arpeggio costs $5.70 for 10 espresso capsules. Folgers Black Silk blend for a K-Cup brewed-coffee machine is $10.69 for 12 pods) you realize you'd be saving money brewing a big pot of the most expensive coffee even if you throw out what you do not drink. So why were people buying more and more of them? Convenience! To many people, the convenience outweighs the cost.

The take away from this is that more than branding strategies facilitate a company's Revenue Stream. It can also be improved and increased by a real understanding of customer behavior. The more efficiently we use CRM to identify, analyze, and recognize customer behavior, the more we can affect Revenue Stream.

Effective CRM strategies and tools facilitate Revenue Stream strategies for companies by allowing you to understand what is important to your Customer Segments. It allows you to build pricing mechanisms you can present to customers in an effort to address what they will pay to get what they need. If you do not think that Revenue Stream strategies directly affect your relationship with customers, consider the most recent struggles banking institutions are experiencing from charging administrative and usage fees to checking account customers. The same is true for companies that charge subscription and licensing fees their customers feel are unfair or that do not provide value to them (like convenience does to the users of the single-cup coffee maker).

If your CRM strategy does not support your Revenue Stream strategies, and your Revenue Stream strategy does not consider how it affects the customer relationship, the mechanisms you use to make money are disconnected. Consider how younger banking customers, while not happy to pay monthly usage fees, would rather pay them than to give up some features (like depositing checks electronically via their mobile device).

KEY RESOURCES:

As firmly stated earlier, the worst mistake any company can make about CRM is to define it primarily in terms of the technology or tools that support it. However, CRM requires Key Resources to make it actionable and useful, just as your business needs them to operate. CRM needs physical, intellectual, human, and financial resources to keep it running as well.

To create a CRM strategy that supports your business (all of your business), you must identify the Key Resources that will support it, including those outside of sales, marketing, and support functions. You must also identify how CRM will support those resources and must be ready to present a business case for how each of the Key Resources of your company will benefit from CRM.

KEY ACTIVITIES:

Every business has a list of the most important things they must do to make its business model work. When a CRM strategy does not align its business processes with the Key Activities that make the business work, it is, in essence, working against it. CRM has the important goal of uplifting the foundational Key Activities of your business with its set of customer relationship activities. Some of these activities may be strictly operational, such as automatically sending a thank you letter to a new customer.

Other activities may be associated directly to how a marketing organization responds to campaigns, or how a sales organization responds to an inquiry, or how a service organization closes a support ticket. CRM activities must always align to the Key Activities a business has established to operate successfully. You will also find that a well-orchestrated CRM strategy will provide business stakeholders with valuable information about the Key Activities customers expect but could be missing from your business processes.

KEY PARTNERSHIPS:

Companies depend on partnerships and alliances to make their business model work. Companies like Walmart and Amazon could not operate without its buyers, suppliers, and distributors. Not all businesses are structured to include external partnerships, but we all depend on internal partnerships to stay in business. CRM best practices encourage companies to disperse silos and work together from a common foundation and strategy for building customer relationships. CRM is at the very core a partnership focused strategy. It is easier to see the value of partnerships when they provide a clear benefit such as distribution efficiency, cost reduction, or geographically strategic positioning. But internal partnerships are a bit more difficult to define. Partnerships, by design, optimize the allocation of resources and activities; internal partnerships are no exception.

If your CRM strategy does not define the role of Key Partners in reducing risk and uncertainty in the customer relationship, as well as include partner-specific tools they will need to support you, your CRM plan will be missing a key strategic component of cooperation and delivery.

COST STRUCTURE:

More CRM efforts go unfunded because sponsors fail to explain how it will support a company's Cost Structure than because they failed to sell the value and attributes of CRM. Creating and delivering value, managing customer relationships and generating revenue for your company cost money. Companies do not make a decision not to invest in CRM because they do not see the importance of their relationships and experiences with clients. Cost-awareness keeps companies from investing in CRM.

Therefore, there must be a strong alignment between CRM and how it supports the company's Cost Structure and business model for reducing cost and driving value. You can sell the value of CRM by aligning with the cost model of your company and providing evidence of the way CRM directly affects cost, value or both.

When leaders listen to presentations about customer relationships and customer experience, the impact on the core building blocks of the business is their first concern. Understanding how CRM supports the business across all of its building blocks, and learning the language and perspective of sponsors and stakeholders, will allow you to have the right conversations at the highest levels of leadership. It will help you show that CRM is there, at every step, orchestrating the actions that strengthen the building blocks of your business.

A PREMATURE OBITUARY

With all of the advances in social media and mobility and the organizational responses to these ground-shifting trends, many people question whether we should still be talking about CRM at all. Some will go as far as proclaiming the death of CRM as a customer strategy. What makes the idea of retiring CRM difficult is that it is truly throwing the baby out with the bathwater. We cannot do away with the basic premise that to win and keep customers we have to have a customer relationship strategy. Customer relationship strategies define the types of people that will benefit from our value proposition. It helps companies determine where and in whom and in what market segments they are going to invest.

It is true that the term has become synonymous with the technology that manages sales force automation, marketing automation, and support automation within the customer lifecycle. Also true is that, in an economy where the customer defines the lifecycle, the engagement, and the channels used to build the relationship, there is an increasing gap between the way the customer engagement happens and the way CRM tools work. The conflict, however, is not over the need for customer relationship management strategies. The question is, "Do we continue to use a term so closely (and mistakenly) associated with technology and software tools?" Even more challenging is the question, "What is the right term to use?" What is a good all-inclusive term that accurately embraces the strategies that help us win and keep customers?

Personally, I am a proponent of using the term "Customer Relationship Strategies" because it points to the "customer" as the entity with whom we want to build the relationship, and it preserves the idea that a "relationship" is the ultimate goal (ideally one where there is a reciprocal perception of value). Using the word relationship connects us back to well-grounded best practices and strategies we have used for generations to build relationships with people. We know that relationships have patterns for growth and deterioration; patterns applicable to customer relationships. What we call the "customer lifecycle" is now non-linear (it does not move nicely from lead generation to opportunity management, to support and loyalty management anymore). We perceived the linear customer lifecycle to represent control over the customer journey, a perception that may have never been accurate, and certainly is not accurate today.

We do an excellent job (both strategic and technology-driven) building functionality and accessibility, which are two of the three rating components that drive people to buy, continue to buy, and recommend you to other people. Customers ask, "Was I able to accomplish what I wanted?" and "Was it easy for me to interact with the company?" The third component (which CRM strategies are not taking into account) is experiential; it is about customers determining how they feel about their interactions with you. Where CRM has traditionally focused on driving the customer journey through workflow, today, empowered by new culture and technology innovation, it is the customer who determines where that journey starts and ends. They choose to purchase, continue to purchase, recommend you, or switch to a competitor based on that experience or combination of experiences.

Nonetheless, the sheer number of attempts to kill and redefine CRM is a testament to its power and flexibility as an engine of business. Attempting to nail it down to "engagement," "experience," or some other term, in an attempt to hide CRM turns it into something you will be unable to successful measure. While some companies spend millions to rename or disconnect themselves from the acronym CRM, its power as a strategy influencing collaboration in every part of the business, and unifying all your customer strategies, remains its greatest strength.

SECTION 3

SPEAKING ABOUT COLLABORATION

CRM IS A COLLABORATIVE EFFORT.
IT REQUIRES YOU ELIMINATE SILOS
ACROSS ALL YOUR BUSINESS
FUNCTIONS.

col·lab·o·rate \ intransitive verb \kə-
'la-bə-rāt\ :to work jointly with others
or together especially in an intellectual
endeavor[4]

"If you want to make peace with your enemy, you have to work with your enemy. Then he becomes your partner."

- Nelson Mandela

An effort like CRM, so crucial to the unification of your company's customer strategies, is going to require honest and heartfelt collaboration. Honest because without fair and straightforward talk about how you are presently building your customer strategies, you will be unable to resolve collaboration problems. Heartfelt because there will be times when the cause of the problem may originate from something done by you or your organization (perhaps not intentionally). A heartfelt, genuine desire to acknowledge problems and move egos aside to resolve them helps you navigate through the difficult conversations you need to have.

CRM is a collaboration strategy. You may not see it as such, but it is. CRM connects you to customers as much as it connects everyone in your company to one another. It can improve your external and internal processes with equal or even greater influence when you collaborate to make it about relationships. Fortunately, some of you already understand this and work for companies that reward collaboration and transparency. I congratulate you!

WHY WE STRUGGLE TO COLLABORATE

For many companies, however, collaborating to make CRM and the customer strategies it supports successful is a tremendous challenge. Even if the effort's sponsor has a budget, a team capable and eager to collaborate and the support of executive leadership, they still have to contend with inherited problems. One of the most common is that, in an effort to resolve immediate problems, organizations often act independently to implement solutions; solutions that later become difficult to undo or integrate with broader customer strategic initiatives. All you have to do is ask around, and the problem/solution explanations become obvious:

- Sales needed a place to manage opportunities.

- Executive leadership needed to gauge the health of the pipeline.

- Marketing needed an efficient way to manage campaigns activities to tie ROI to sales.

- Support needed to modernize their case management capabilities.

- The new website needed a more accessible way for customers to change information, communicate issues, or get feedback from other customers.

There are legitimate concerns about what CRM will accomplish from both managers and employees. Concerns about how CRM could change how they conduct business on a daily basis. Empathy for the needs of each department and the organization as a whole, coupled with the needs of the individuals implementing the practices, can lead to profitable dialog on how to make CRM successful for everyone. It is common to see CRM as the pet project of someone with power or someone who brought the concept from their previous company. Or as something managers do to create reports and dashboards that do nothing for anyone but the company's top executives. Not unlike other technical implementation initiatives, some of the friction over CRM comes from people feeling that they were left out of the process altogether. This perception is accurate much too often and is usually the result of poor collaboration and lack of company-wide participation in customer advocacy efforts. For the most part, the leaders charged with making CRM initiatives successful have the same concerns as the rest of the company. Their concerns are more about supporting the nine business building blocks we discussed earlier. They are focused on keeping the business profitable and, in some extreme cases, keeping the doors open for business. Unless the people running the company and the people implementing their initiatives collaborate to connect the value of CRM to the business goals and support it enthusiastically, CRM cannot succeed.

COLLABORATION IS THE ONLY ALTERNATIVE

Reports from Forrester Research Inc. show that companies that follow best practices for high-level sponsorship, end-user adoption, and usability, and those who consistently stay the course when it comes to developing and rolling out CRM projects across the organization, are succeeding. The Forrester study, supported by more recent studies, drew from interviews with executives at 22 large North American companies to learn about their CRM successes. All 22 saw increased revenues, lower costs, higher ROI and improved competitive strength, thanks to following CRM best practices that include:

- Strong executive sponsorship of the program

- CRM leadership collaboration with IT

- A governance structure that fosters accountability and decision-making across the entire company

- Customer-focused defined objectives and processes in place, before applying the right technology

- Following a realistic pace for the rollout

As summarized by Bill Band, the Forrester report's project leader, staying the course together is one of the most important lessons for CRM success:

"The companies [in the study] all said they developed a long-term vision and did one country at a time, one function at a time… 'CRM in 90 days, implemented and done,' that is a fallacy. It speaks to the over-hype in early '90s when people had visions of quick and easy return, and it's just not there."

I wish that everyone could see things from my vantage point. It is a position that allows me to step back and see the hard work and even personal struggles that the entire company goes through to care for customers. The company executives are expected to work together to assess and implement strategies and technologies appropriate to the goals and needs of the company. Meanwhile, department heads work hard to manage their teams, either empowered or encumbered by the same leaders, to meet objectives that are more customer-focused.

CRM can be a bridge between both goals, empowering people across the company to deliver exceptional customer experiences. Sales, operations, marketing, and service leaders can form a powerful partnership, leveraging common goals. Company goals often go unrealized because they do not include a strategy to collaborate with employees. First line employees obtain invaluable insight feedback directly from the customer. When excluded, employees develop their own goals and processes to help customers. While your CEO looks for better client retention insight, your call center agents are busy doing what they can to keep customers happy. In the absence of a process or tool to help people do both, each side will create their own (often disconnected) solutions. While the Chief Operations Officer is busy trying to reduce the time customers wait on the phone, the customer service specialist is listening empathetically to the mom who needs as much of his time to find a same-day appointment for her sick child. Without collaboration the people investing in CRM and the people implementing it work against each other without intending to. Without collaboration, the customer ultimately walks away feeling that you are not working together to help them with their needs and making it easy for them to do business with you.

To create and deploy the correct strategy and technology that helps companies win and keep customers, you have to collaborate. The people who make the decisions, the people who use the technology, the people who interact with customers, the people who provide them service, the people who help customers feel rewarded for doing business with you, the people who collaborate daily with one another to meet customer needs... they ALL have to work together to enjoy success together.

THE CRM EYE EXAM

I have never enjoyed the yearly trip to the eye doctor. It is not the actual exam that irritates me, but the number of people involved. One person checks my records and signs me in; another performs the pre-exam before the optometrist takes me into the examination room and sits me on "the big chair." There he will get uncomfortably close to my face, shine a light that must have been designed for use with lighthouses in the Eastern seaboard, and switch suspiciously similar lenses in front of me to determine if I can see better with one or two.... one, or two. Then, as I stumble blindly back into the reception area with giant dilated pupils, yet another person begins the process of helping me select contact lenses and frames.

Last year I noticed something that had escaped me in previous years. When Denise, the eye care technician, takes me to the "great wall of frames" to choose my frames, she always asks me to take off my glasses. What follows is the ridiculous exercise of making decisions about what I look like in the new frames without being able to see. Seems a little crazy, but we all do it. We make decisions about our eyewear while wearing frames providing no vision at all. It is no surprise that, when the frames come back with the correct lenses, our opinion of them is so different. Lately, I have been taking my wife with me for an unbiased opinion. Even Denise jumps in and shares her thoughts, and ultimately the decision I make is far more educated and unbiased. This collaboration has saved me from embarrassing myself many times. I know that making the decision about these new glasses falls on me. I have to decide how they will fit my lifestyle and allow me to interact with my world, and the people I bring into it. It is a lot easier, though, to choose when I recruit help (especially when my vision is unclear).

I have come to appreciate, when my vision is weak and obstructed, that the collaborative effort of helping me with my vision, works best when the right people get involved. That's when I can count on every person involved in this process to help me correct my vision, maintain that healthy vision, and select the right tools for keeping my vision clear.

I shared this analogy with a friend recently and she told me that a major retailer of eyewear in the United States has a system that photographs you wearing the frames of your choosing, and then allows you to look at pictures of yourself wearing them. Another retailer allows you to upload pictures and do the same thing online before you even get to the store. There is even a "Style Survey" that lets you choose glasses that fit your personality: "What is your idea of a dream vacation?" "Which shoes best reflect your style?" "What's your idea of a perfect night out?" A very helpful system, but only a part of a larger process because frames do not improve your eyesight, but make it easier for you to wear your glasses. They are only a part of the equation that allows you to apply individuality and style to a vital need, the need to see properly. Incidentally, this is a fitting comparison to the way some companies focus on the selection of CRM technology and stylish marketing websites without a focus on what they are intended to do for customers.

The correct approach to correcting and improving your vision is to work together to examine the myopic and nearsighted vision that affects your business as a team with unique perspectives and roles and answers. And yes that includes the people that help you look good in those jazzy spectacles, and as an imperative, the customer.

Some of you reading this are preparing to try on some new eyeglasses. Some of you are regretting the set you already chose.

Some of you are realizing you never even bothered to get your vision checked. As with my visit to the eye doctor, it always helps to have the right people involved who understand what to check. That help must come from people within your company who can impartially provide vision corrections and simultaneously consider the importance of the voice of the customer and how they see you.

SOLVING CRM COLLABORATION PROBLEMS

Only through collaboration can we resolve problems that fall under what author Craig Weber defines as "adaptive challenges." In his book "Conversational Capacity,"[5] Craig writes about both "routine" problems and "adaptive" problems saying:

"Routine problems may be painful, expensive, and frustrating, but we have the advantage of knowing what to do about them and how to work through them. We have, in other words, a routine for dealing with them. Contrast a routine problem with an adaptive challenge. An adaptive challenge is a problem for which we have no ready solution, no expert we can call upon to guide us through, no clear way forward. We have, in other words, no routine. We know we're facing an adaptive challenge when we find ourselves in unfamiliar territory with no mental map of our predicament. Lost in uncharted terrain, we must pull together with the people around us to make sense of the hard realities we're facing and successfully adapt to the new environment."

In "Dilemmas in a General Theory of Planning,"[6] urban planners Horst Rittel and Melvin Webber talk about problems that are "ill-defined" by calling them "wicked problems." Wicked problems are those that do not have a definable and separable solution. Wicked problems are, well, never solved. At best, they are only resolved over and again. Rittel and Webber were specifically addressing the challenges involved in making decisions within immensely complex social circumstances (such as the decision-making required to achieve sound public policy or urban design). They also used the term to expand on the problems that face interdisciplinary collaboration. Collaboration is a wicked problem because , as Rittel and Webber define it, collaboration has no definitive preparation; it has no common rules, no ultimate test for the solution and each collaboration yields its own specific and fitted results. With collaboration, we learn with each trial and error, and each attempt is significant in contributing to the solutions we forge together. Each collaboration is unique and without limits for the number of benefits it can yield.

Why am I telling you all this, knowing that companies spend thousands of dollars a year to motive employees to work as a team to resolve problems? Because team building alone is not the answer. The challenges you face will never reach resolution unless you collaborate through sometimes painful realizations about how little you actually know about the customer. Each collaboration must yield its own specific and fitted results to build strategies that help you know the customer better. The dose of realism you must inject into your customer efforts RIGHT NOW is that too many people are making decisions about the customer without seeing the customer as a whole.

There is a poem I love which makes this point in a fabulous and inspirational way. So if you will indulge me... Here is "The Blind Men and the Elephant" by John Godfrey Saxe (1816-1887):

It was six men of Indostan
To learning much inclined,
Who went to see the Elephant
(Though all of them were blind),
That each by observation
Might satisfy his mind.

The First approached the Elephant,
And happening to fall
Against his broad and sturdy side,
At once began to bawl:
"God bless me! but the Elephant
Is very like a WALL!"

The Second, feeling of the tusk,
Cried, "Ho, what have we here,
So very round and smooth and sharp?

To me 'tis mighty clear
This wonder of an Elephant
Is very like a SPEAR!"

The Third approached the animal,
And happening to take
The squirming trunk within his hands,
Thus boldly up and spake:
"I see," quoth he, "the Elephant
Is very like a SNAKE!"

The Fourth reached out an eager hand,
And felt about the knee
"What most this wondrous beast is like
Is mighty plain," quoth he:
"'Tis clear enough the Elephant
Is very like a TREE!"

The Fifth, who chanced to touch the ear,
Said: "E'en the blindest man
Can tell what this resembles most;
Deny the fact who can,
This marvel of an Elephant
Is very like a FAN!"

The Sixth no sooner had begun
About the beast to grope,
Than seizing on the swinging tail

That fell within his scope,
"I see," quoth he, "the Elephant
Is very like a ROPE!"

And so these men of Indostan
Disputed loud and long,
Each in his own opinion
Exceeding stiff and strong,
Though each was partly in the right,
And all were in the wrong!

The most tragic flaw in your customer-centered strategies may be that you do not have a clear picture of what your customer actually looks like. You formulate your opinions based on a partial view and limited knowledge of customers without a comprehensive understanding that can only come from your collective knowledge of the customer. It raises questions about how people who have an incomplete picture of the customer can make customer relationship, engagement, or experience management decisions without meaningful collaborations across the company. We speak so boldly about an elephant we have never seen entirely.

CRM success requires that you work together to identify the routine and solve the adaptive. You have to work together to understand the problems that are most usual in your interactions with customers, and (through the support of the right analytics) learn what causes them, when, and how people throughout your company are resolving them. Likewise, you have to collaborate to respond to adaptive challenges. These are more difficult to address because, by definition, adaptive challenges are those for which we do not have a process. An unmanaged adaptive challenge can kill your business and requires that everyone put aside their differences and even admit to creating the problem. Collaborating on the strategy and practice of CRM is indeed a "wicked problem." It surfaces challenges and discussions with people from multiple skill sets, competencies, agendas, and goals that sometimes seem insurmountable and results in wounded egos and challenging conversations.

LEVERAGING COLLABORATIVE CIRCLES

One of the best ways to engage collaboratively with the customer challenges CRM solves is through what Michael P. Farrell refers to as "collaborative circles" in his book "Collaborative Circles: Friendship Dynamics and Creative Work:"[7]

"A collaborative circle is a set of peers in the same discipline who, through the open exchange of support, ideas, and criticism develop into an interdependent group with a common vision that guides their creative work."

"Creative work is rarely done by a lone genius. Artists, writers, scientists and other professionals often do their most creative work when collaborating within a circle of like-minded friends. Experimenting together and challenging one another, they develop the courage to rebel against the established traditions in their field. Working alone or in pairs, then meeting as a group to discuss their emerging ideas, they forge a new, shared vision that guides their work. When circles work well, the unusual interactions that occur in them draw out creativity in each of the members."

With CRM, however, rather than restricting participation to like-minds and people with complementing competencies, the collaboration circle we are talking about is a "sharing circle." One in which you share what you know about the customer to help others paint a complete picture. The types of conversations you have today to make CRM tools available to sales, marketing, and support are part of one circle. In that circle, you talk about the customer as an individual about whom you are collecting information. You talk about the customer in its relational form so that you can connect information about them from the right sources, in a manner that keeps that information secured and free of duplicates. Those are important conversations in your circle if your role is to implement a CRM tool. But unless you understand how each person in your company interacts with the customer, how they take care of customer needs, what challenges they experience in creating a positive customer experience, then your view of the customer is incomplete. You have to collaborate with the people that can help complete that picture. You have to expand your circles.

CRM collaboration cannot amount to a bunch of meaningless tasks in a CRM implementation project plan. Here is where we often realize that we have to talk to people throughout the company to design the business processes that will drive CRM workflow. Here is also where many of the contributors to that analysis learn for the first time that a CRM project is even in progress. CRM collaboration cannot take place in isolation in corporate boardrooms where executives decide the reports they need to run the business without feedback from the people physically interacting with the customer. It cannot happen without an understanding of customer needs from the customer himself.

CRM collaboration cannot fix internal business process challenges if it leaves out the people for whom CRM was created (and I am talking about the customer, not sales). It cannot be something you do strictly for the sake of improving operational efficiencies unless it improves the customer experience and is connected to all the people creating that experience. As Jeremy Bentham put it, "It is the greatest good to the greatest number of people which is the measure of right and wrong." As Spock would say, "The needs of the many outweigh the needs of the few."

RETIRING THE SILOS

Wikipedia reports that at its peak in 1967, the stockpile of nuclear warheads owned by the Unites States came to an alarming

31,265 warheads. It is estimated that, since 1945, the United States produced more than 70,000 nuclear warheads, which is more than all other nuclear weapon states combined. The Soviet Union/Russia has built approximately 55,000 nuclear warheads since 1949, France built 1110 warheads since 1960, the United Kingdom built 835 warheads since 1952, China built about 600 warheads since 1964, and other nuclear powers built less than 500 warheads altogether since they developed their first nuclear weapons.[8] There are thousands of nuclear silos all over the world (active and inactive), yet, the Oxford English Dictionary uses the following examples first to help explain what a "silo" is:

"It's vital that team members step out of their silos and start working together [AS MODIFIER]: we have made significant strides in breaking down that silo mentality."

"Most companies have expensive IT systems they have developed over the years, but they are siloed. Why are so many companies still silo-ing their SEO and social media marketing?"

"Managers have been told to break down the walls between siloed applications."

The "silo" mentality is a common and devastating problem we face every day. You create them when you refuse (intentionally or unintentionally) to share information with others. This mentality reduces operational efficiency, collaboration, and even morale.

It is no coincidence that customer-related silos (as I am about to describe them) align perfectly with the seven relationship components I described earlier (definition, engagement, centricity, service, support, transparency, and experience). In the absence of someone managing a specific relationship component, someone else will step in to address the deficiency. Customers will demand it and the organizations within your company that pick up on the need will respond to support them in one or more areas. Unfortunately, when companies do this in isolation, they create silos that duplicate these efforts:

CUSTOMER RELATIONSHIP SILOS:

Contributing to a centralized view of customers' worries salespeople because they fear someone else will sell to their prospects or intrude on a relationship they have worked so hard to establish. When salespeople keep customer activity and information to themselves, it creates blind spots in what should be a 360-degree view of the customer. The concern with sharing contact information is not a strategy or technology problem. It is a trust problem that requires attention. If you cannot trust the people you work with to exchange information openly and collaboratively, you will never be able to enjoy the benefits a unified customer strategy offers.

From a strictly practical perspective, it benefits everyone to know what is happening with a customer, regardless of where they are in the sales cycle. Especially if they are an existing customer already receiving marketing information or serviced by the customer service organization. The stories you hear about sales professionals calling on customers, only to find out the customer is angry with your company, are true. Of greater concern than sharing information with your peers is that your customers are engaging your company via many channels and talking about it (maybe even about you) via social media. Working with all the organizations that own customer interactions and channels, the people engaging customers via social conversations, and those gathering important information about the customer (their buying preferences, expectations, and experiences with your company) is more important than ever.

CRM may only be your opportunity and pipeline management system today. Today it may only be your strategy for qualifying, pursuing leads and closing sales. With the right collaborations, CRM can become about truly knowing your customers. The right collaboration strategy can be your best resource for maintaining an accurate record of customer data and their interactions with your company, regardless of who they interact with at your company or where they go to learn or talk about you.

You must include the people and organizations involved in building relationship definition and expectation management in the CRM collaboration.

CUSTOMER ENGAGEMENT SILOS:

Elsewhere in your company, another group of people is defining how customers will engage you and via what channels. Customer Engagement Strategies evaluate the most cost effective communication channels for customers to reach you and how. A strong Customer Engagement strategy also continually evaluates what channels your customers want to use to reach you. Where CRM and CEM often disconnect is in the implementation of supporting tools. CEM tools are most often implemented by call center organizations in support of customer service and support functions. It is common for sales and marketing organizations to use different tools from those used by customer service due to the complexity and investment required to implement CEM tools. While CRM tools are commonly just software, CEM tools that support the call center require interactive voice response, external customer portals, knowledge management, chat, and messaging resources.

Engagement, however, is not just about tools and it most certainly does not just happen in contact centers or call centers. Engagement is every email, call, chat, or conversation you have with customers or about customers. Engagement is everything that holds the customer's attention, any communication that invites them to participate in an interaction, and every channel you use to interlock their attention. Engagement is anything that allows you and the customer to evaluate the value your relationship brings, and the security of that relationship continuing to exist.

You must include the people and organizations involved in building communication and engagement channels in the CRM collaboration.

CUSTOMER-CENTRICITY SILOS:

Over the past few years, the term "customer-centricity" has gained a lot of popularity. It is used to describe CRM and even replace the term. In many companies, customer-centricity is a marketing-owned activity for customer segmentation and identification. However, customer-centricity is not a replacement term for CRM. And it is not just marketing's responsibility.

Author and CRM expert Don Peppers explains it this way in a recent post on his LinkedIn blog:

"What does it mean to be 'customer-centric' as a business? Assuming that you start with a quality product and service, being customer-centric means understanding the customer's point of view and respecting the customer's interest. You fix problems, handle complaints, and remember individual customer preferences. But customer-centric competition starts with an individual customer and tries to meet as many of that customer's needs as possible – across all the company's divisions and business units, and through time (i.e., meeting a customer's needs week after week, month after month)."

Customer-centricity is not a strategy disjointed from CRM. It is the component of the CRM strategy that addresses the individual needs and preferences of customers. It is the personalization of the customer experience; what you do that makes them feel that you are thinking about them and their needs specifically. Making the customer central to your business is not all customer centricity is about. The customer already IS the center of your business. I find it interesting that the Greek word from which we derive the English word "centric" is the word "kentrikos" or "of the center," which comes from the word "kentron" or "center." In other words, the customer is already the center of our business and the things that are "of the customer" are customer centric. I respect the position of several fellow authors who use the term "customer centricity" to express the need for companies to identify their best customers; those in whom they will invest. That determination, within the seven unified customer strategies introduced in this book, happens at the customer relationship definition stage. Customer centricity is the strategy that focuses on the needs and behavior most important to the customer so that we can customize and personalize their experiences.

You must include the people and organizations personalizing customer experiences in the CRM collaboration.

CUSTOMER SERVICE SILOS:

You cannot separate the concepts of "relationship" and "service" without diminishing the potential for a genuine relationship. Yet many CRM strategies are implemented without serious consideration for what "customer service" actually is. For many CRM practitioners, service is just a modular component of the CRM software application. It is something you implement if the Customer Service manager of your company is interested or if you have enough budget.

Too often we overlook the idea that "customer service" is an essential part of what CRM does. Not because people don't know what customer service is, but because they view customer service as a function and not a customer strategy that gives all the other customer strategies a charter for how to treat the customer. Customer service strategies are not just for call centers. They are for all of us. It is the set of rules we put in place that says "this is how we will treat the customer, and this is what we will do to correct things when we don't treat them in accordance with our commitment." The definition of "customer services" has gradually disconnected from the definition of "service" and the idea that the "customer" is the recipient of that service. Instead, "customer service" has become synonymous with the practices call centers use to manage their interactions with customers and the metrics that make it cost-effective to interact with them. We have created call center metrics that determine how long an agent should be on the phone and have created tools for moving the customer to more self-help activities. As a result, we detached "service" from "customer service" and today we struggle to maintain these call center success measurements while trying to deliver good customer experiences. It has become difficult for one side of your company to use call center metrics to gauge success while another measures it based on customer experience. One side pushes call center agents to make their interactions with customers as brief as possible while the other tells them to give the customer what they need, no matter how long it takes.

Service is contributing to the welfare of others. One of my favorite people and the Customer Experience Officer for one of the world's leading footwear brands, has a quote on her signature block from Rabindranath Tagore:

"I slept and dreamt that life was joy. I awoke and saw that life was service. I acted and behold, service was joy."

Customer service is the strategy that brings joy with structure to all your customer strategies. It makes everyone follow the same rules for caring about your customers and tells you what you should do for them when they are not happy. It enables everyone in your company to give customers memorable experiences, and it empowers them to do what they can to meet their expectations.

You must include the people and organizations involved in meeting service promises and commitments in the front lines in the CRM collaboration.

CUSTOMER EXPERIENCE SILOS:

The most recent culprit in our "silos" list is the concept of "customer experience." Evaluating the customer experience is, by far, one of the most effective ways for your company to understand what your customers need from you. It is an indispensable part of winning and keeping customers. For companies that have experienced unsuccessful CRM implementations, or for companies that fear CRM failure, it is easy to see customer experience as the ultimate answer. Companies that shift their attention exclusively to customer experience risk isolating the strategies that support it and feed it with necessary information and processes. I am amongst the strongest supporters of adopting customer experience measurements to assess the health of customer relationships. I am also amongst the most avid to emphasize that customer experience is a measurement we use. It is not a strategy we build independently from the customer relationship, engagement, centricity, service, and experience strategies that jointly give you a realistic view of customers.

You must include the people and organizations involved in customer experience measurement and planning in the CRM collaboration.

The right feedback by the right people can more efficiently define what you need, and ideally, helps you deliver the strategies and tools you need to serve others with greater passion and ability (both inside and outside your company).

When people work together to implement CRM, it allows it to become the foundation of a new imperative described by Harley Manning and Kerry Bodine in the book "Outside In:"[9]

"...creating and nurturing a system of interdependent, self-reinforcing practices that align employee, partners, processes, policies, and technology around customers."

To finish the CRM race, we have to run together, arm in arm. We have to set aside our agendas and collaborate on common goals that take into account the needs of all CRM stakeholders and, most importantly, the customer.

SECTION 4

SPEAKING ABOUT RESOLUTION

CRM REQUIRES TRANSPARENCY.
THE CHALLENGES IT UNVEILS
MUST BE SOLVED THROUGH
HONEST COMMUNICATION.

res·o·lu·tion \ noun \ ˌre-zə-ˈlü-shən\: the act or process of dealing with something successfully: to progress from dissonance to consonance[10]

"It is easy to dodge our responsibilities, but we cannot dodge the consequences of dodging our responsibilities."

- Sir Josiah Stamp

K nowing where the silos are will help you recruit the people that will help you implement the strategies, processes, and technology that leads to strong customer relationships and experiences. However, simply choosing to work together does not solve the challenges companies experience when they launch a CRM strategy or project. It requires resolve and determination, and more importantly the knowledge to execute. CRM is worth doing and "whatever is worth doing at all is worth doing well" (Philip Stanhope, 4th Earl of Chesterfield). Implementing the right customer relationship strategies and tools require the type of determination that leads to open and honest dialog. The process requires the people making company-wide decisions about the business and the people enforcing and implementing those decisions to resolve their differences and answer questions that affect them both. Having a successful business means making tough choices, including those that make certain everyone adheres to the practices that keep the business running and in compliance with the law. The people selling, marketing, and supporting the business have a responsibility to follow those guidelines while maintaining a focus on creating positive customer experiences. The correct dialog allows you to address the problems that are interfering with how you run your business as well as how you take care of customers.

You already know that communication is the foundation of a strong business. However, we are talking about more than just sharing information and distributing it across the company. We are talking about having an open dialog that facilitates asking the right questions from the right people; allowing everyone in your business to offer their feedback without fear of judgment or retribution. CRM efforts that do not start with frank conversations lead to almost immediate performance problems and mistrust. Something as simple as overlooking introductory dialog about your goals for the CRM effort can result in suspicion, animosity, and even resentments. Especially when the people excluded have done this well at other companies and feel you are not accounting for their valuable feedback. The disconnect between what we call "communication" and true, genuine, open dialog, accounts for the failure of many CRM implementations. It is ironic that, as it relates to CRM technology implementation specifically, we spend so much time deploying the technology and so little time talking to the people who will use it. We complain that the CRM project failed from a lack of user acceptance, then try desperately to correct the problem by initiating dialog with people who, by this point, feel that you overlooked them.

I intentionally use the word "resolution" because this must be the goal of our customer relationship conversations:

1. To engage in dialog that helps us deal with problems successfully;

2. To progress from dissonance (lack of harmony) to consonance (agreement or compatibility between opinions or actions).

Your response will make you part of the solution or part of the problem; a facilitator of dissonance or harmony. Your attitude will make CRM an instrument of unification or division. If you believe in isolating your efforts to communicate with others, you will create disunion. You will keep your customer strategies in a state of dissonance with one another and will continue to exclude potential contributors. If you choose instead to engage everyone who serves the customer in transparent dialog, you will discover real problems to solve.

I want you to do something incredibly courageous and which could potentially save you thousands, perhaps millions of dollars. I want you to start calling the people within your company who interact with customers every day. I want you to ask them two simple yet penetrating questions:

1. What are the most important problems we need to solve for our customers?

2. How are you solving these problems today?

Gather a strong sample of answers and compare them. Be sure to ask a representative sample from throughout your entire company. You may find that your goals for CRM and the problems that really need solving are not the same. I have asked hundreds of leaders to perform this inquiry with amazing results and a change in their perspective on the value of solving problems together.

I repeatedly use the expression "the people who make customers feel rewarded for doing business with you." It is a term that came from the book "How To Win Customers and Keep Them For Life" by Dr. Michael LeBoeuf whose mentoring and friendship motivated a lot of my writing. If you have not read his book, I strongly encourage you to do so. It is the foundation of what most customer service authors have taught us in the last fifteen years. Michael's statement is powerful because it acknowledges that your employees and partners are creating a sense of value for your customers. They make customers feel that you are rewarding them rather than penalizing them for doing business with you. Employees and partners know more than anyone about the engagement, functionality, accessibility, and brand connection problems your customers experience. Your complications implementing the right solutions to customer problems originate more often from the questions you are not asking the people who know customers best.

One of my most favorite reads is the book "Why Employees Don't Do What They're Supposed To Do and What To Do About It," by Ferdinand F. Fournies. Human resource professionals quote it often because of its usefulness in determining why people do not perform as expected. The book lists the following reasons why people do not do what they are supposed to do at work:

1. They don't know why they should do it

2. They don't know how to do it

3. They don't know what they are supposed to do

4. They think your way will not work

5. They think their way is better

6. They think something else is more important

7. There is no positive consequence to them for doing it

8. They think they are doing it

9. They are rewarded for not doing it

10. They are punished for doing what they are supposed to do

11. They anticipate a negative consequence for doing it

12. There is no negative consequence to them for poor performance

13. Obstacles beyond their control

14. Their personal limits prevent them from performing

15. Personal problems

16. No one could do it

Fournies' list describes fittingly many of the reasons people do not support customer initiatives like CRM. Sometimes people do not see pass their priorities, needs, or inter-departmental agendas, regardless of whether they are doing so because they want to isolate themselves or because they don't know any better. Thinking that everyone will support CRM or will simply get behind the effort because a senior executive mandates it is a dangerous assumption. People respond differently based on their knowledge of the effort and their ability to respond (based on what they think they should do or are already doing). You have to work together to inventory what people need in order to respond adequately to many of the questions I have asked you so far.

Every customer relationship initiative is different and may require more extensive investigation of the apprehensions people have about it. If you present yourself as a trustworthy advocate for both employees and customers, people will be more inclined to tell you their concerns. Eventually, they will actively include you in the conversations they are already having. Especially as it pertains to new efforts, employees and partners are going to have many questions you must be ready to answer before they commit fully.

Here are some of the most important ones:

WHY ARE YOU DOING THIS?

People want to know the answer to a very important question, "Why?" Why the expense, why the change in a new direction that could disrupt day-to-day work life? Why now? "Why" questions are fair and reasonable from the people who will be called upon to carry the flag and make sacrifices to make CRM a success. It is also a question that helps you validate the reason you are doing this to begin with and one that you have to answer well. Addressing why you are implementing a customer relationship strategy, or technology solution is the first part of this exercise. The second part is to listen to what happens next. It may be that people welcome your explanations with open arms. In companies that did not do their due diligence to understand what solutions were already in place, this could result instead in some unpleasant surprises. It could result in learning that there are efforts in place that will not allow you to proceed as planned. It could also be there is a history you do not know; the story of why CRM failed in the past and how people with a need to access customer information created their "own way." You may hear about the creative and innovative ways people fixed the problem, and you may get an opportunity to build that collaboration we have been talking so much about by identifying champions and subject matter experts.

For many of you reading this book, CRM is not a new thing. Not by far! You have been at multiple companies and used several different CRM solutions that have the words dynamics and act and force, or the name of mythical horses in their name. You have seen them succeed and fail. You have created, by now, personal preferences for the ones you like using best. With that experience, you have also gained insight into the many (sometimes ridiculous reasons) why companies choose to implement CRM. Some of you are asking the "why" question about your current company. Why did they do this? What was the long-term goal and what is the plan to leverage such a vital initiative for gaining company-wide intelligence about customer interactions? The answers to "why CRM?" cannot be only about centralizing contact records or having a place to manage your sales activity and pipeline. Not because CRM does not perform these tasks well, but because people know what CRM can do and how it can help you target the right customers with the right value proposition using very powerful tools.

You have to be ready to explain "why" CRM will support the other strategies in the customer strategy universe (engagement, centricity, service, transparency, and experience), as well as the customer experience ecosystem itself. People need to know how your CRM strategy accounts for what they are already doing to win and keep customers, and how it aligns (or doesn't) with the things they are already doing.

WHY SHOULD WE BE A PART OF IT?

Gaining people's attention does not always mean winning their enthusiasm. Besides knowing why you are doing something, they also want to know why they should support it. Remember that CRM projects, in general, already have bad reputations for low user adoption. CRM applications have been around long enough for even people who have never used them to know they have been the target of criticism. Why, then, should people jump for joy to support an effort few have implemented successfully? ...Allegedly. It is not difficult to help people understand why they should support customer relationship efforts. People know that the customer is the reason you are in business and why you come to work every day. If you don't believe that, or have difficulty getting your team to believe it, read the "Speaking About the Customer" section of this book and then come back. The goal is to help people understand that CRM is a foundational part of how your company will identify the customers you can best serve. It is part of how you create memorable experiences that bring them back and motivate them to recommend you to others.

The endeavor you are asking people to support is not a software implementation effort, a technology project or business process automation effort. Even if that is the next step in the CRM strategy, you cannot make it all about software tools. You are asking them to be part of a better and more intimate way to know the customer. You are building a road that accelerates how your customers engage you, how sales identify what customers want from you, and how well you are meeting the commitments you made to them as a transparent brand. If people see CRM only as software, they will add it to the list of other things your company is implementing, and part of a longer list of things that disrupt their ability to care for customers. Participation and (better yet) collaboration requires that you align your goals and roadmap for implementing CRM with what people are already doing. You will watch many of the tasks you thought you had to initiate yourself already live and in progress by your new advocates.

ARE YOU GOING TO TEACH ME
HOW TO DO THIS SUCCESSFULLY?

I started my CRM career many years ago as a software trainer. The software company I worked for had a fabulous catalog of certification programs we offered to users, developers, and system administrators. CRM software companies have improved software application training to make it contextual to the experience of using the software itself. Learning the tools that help you win customers is an essential part of CRM, and you have plenty of great training resources, training companies, and trainers to leverage in your CRM software education journey.

We are talking, however about more than software training here. We are talking about skills beyond the tools and knowledge preliminary to anything you teach and learn about CRM implementation. People need to know that you have a plan for educating them in the fundamentals of CRM practice and that you will give them the skills they need to make it applicable to their areas of focus. People need to know that you plan to educate them about what customer relationship strategy is, how it helps your business, and how you will leverage it (with their help) to mobilize the processes that help them help customers. People ultimately want to know you have a plan for addressing knowledge deficiencies without putting their current efforts in jeopardy.

WHAT IS OUR ROLE?

People do not want to receive marching orders disconnected from their understanding of the larger CRM initiative. That is often the case when project managers treat people as a "task assignment" in a project plan. People want to know the role they will have in molding the strategy as stakeholders before you tell them what you expect them to contribute, to whom, when and where. Defining the role of individuals and teams in relationship to the "big picture" is extremely critical to collaboration. Helping people understand their role (or better yet, their contribution) creates a connection between what they may be doing in isolation and the greater good.

It is no accident that this book addresses the problem of business silos and challenges of building collaboration first. Ambiguity about how you may be using technology to eliminate jobs is dangerous. No one wants to be left wondering if their job is at risk or if you plan to replace processes they need to do their job, at least not without their involvement. No player ever goes into a ball game wondering what position he or she will play and how his or her contribution will help win the game. Successful CRM strategies account for every player at every stage of the game and plan adequately for their involvement.

WHY IS "THIS" A PRIORITY?

To many people, CRM is sometimes a pipe dream that interferes with their job. As a result, they face conflicting priorities. Is it their contribution to the CRM effort or doing their job? To the salesperson that has to meet his quota by end of the quarter, the customer service representative that has to meet service level agreements, and the call center manager who has pressing utilization and call center metrics to support, CRM is but "another" unreasonable change coming down to them from the "people upstairs."

There is perhaps no greater "reality check" to a business initiative than when you have to answer why something is a priority. Companies implement CRM for many wrong reasons that have nothing to do with what should be a priority. The "need" for dashboards and reports often put the things that matter most at the mercy of the things that matter least. I am not saying reports and dashboards are not important. I am saying that they are not always the right reason to implement CRM, especially at the expense of more urgent things like understanding customer needs or serving the customer. You have to be ready to answer why CRM is a priority. Fortunately, this book presents compelling reasons for making CRM foundational to the customer initiatives that should be a priority for your business.

WHY IS "THIS" INITIATIVE GOING TO WORK?

Remember that you may not be the only person within your company advocating the value of their initiative. People may be in the middle of other types of business and technology transitions (personnel changes, policy implementations, system and hardware upgrades, etc.). As a result, they face conflicting priorities about what is most important (their contribution to the CRM effort, another IT project, or doing their job). CRM can serve as a vehicle to connect all your efforts to win and retain customers through positive customer experiences, but you have to communicate CRM value effectively. CRM is not a rest stop in the customer experience journey. It is part of the core infrastructure of a company's customer acquisition and retention strategy.

Just in the last five years, companies have introduced more new strategy approaches for CRM, change management, self-service, quality management, and enterprise planning than we have seen in the previous ten years combined. The same is true about the introduction of hardware and software technology innovation more advanced that anything we have seen in the past twenty years. It makes sense that, at this pace, you may have to fight for attention (even more so if some things did not launch with the anticipated success). Do not be surprised that some people approach CRM as another idea in a long line of failed efforts and be prepared to state your case.

SUSPEND YOUR UNBELIEF

If you are tasked with contributing to the CRM effort in any way, you share equal accountability in this matter. While your executives are responsible for engaging you in meaningful dialog that helps answer your questions and allow you to contribute your experiences, you are responsible for your part. We all have to stop acting like combatants and start acting like partners willing to share information and bring issues to final resolution. It is your support and contribution to your company's CRM effort that will make it a success. For those of you in the middle of a CRM crisis, you have a choice to either invigorate a failing effort or speed its demise.

While it is true that CRM success expectations are low for some, it is also true that thousands of companies worldwide experience a high return on their CRM investment. Many companies achieve their goal of improving the lives of the people and the customers they serve by implementing CRM as part of a unified strategy. Every company has unique needs. Perhaps that is why it can be difficult to pin down CRM success and failure statistics – because no one single CRM effort is the same. So suspend your disbelief until you understand what your company is doing and the goals it has set.

Because CRM has been around for a while, there is a large enough test sample population from which to draw case studies. If you ask questions, you will get answers. Seek out the forums that talk about CRM implementations, good and bad. Visit your industry water coolers and engage personally with the people who have gone through your situation.

TAKE OWNERSHIP

Approaching this effort with a positive and enthusiastic attitude does not mean that you agree with everything you hear. It means that you are willing to provide honest feedback and not purposely sabotage the efforts of the people trying to help it succeed. CRM is a living thing that you can deploy gradually to address the greatest needs of the company. In some cases, it may be best to deploy a centralized, unified strategy across the entire company simultaneously. In either case, there will be some sacrifices needed from all the stakeholders. Be willing to listen to all proposed approaches and have an open mind about the impact it may have on you.

INCREASE THE DIALOG

This book is a tool to promote and increase the dialog that must take place between the people leading the CRM process and the people helping to make it successful. Sometimes a company approaches CRM with the best of intentions but still hurts the people it is supposed to help. Through the questions we discussed so far, you can clarify and correct hindrances to communication and achieve mutually beneficial results. Sometimes the people in charge are unable or unwilling to initiate the dialog. In such cases, I encourage you to initiate. Ask others about what they have heard. Engage in conversations about what you have learned about CRM and how it can help your company, then make every effort to talk to your leadership. Offer your support and be open to reviewing and discussing the questions we listed in this section.

If your company is talking about CRM at any level, and they have not initiated a conversation with you, take the time to initiate the dialog yourself. Especially if your company is in the process of selecting a CRM technology partner, be aggressive in initiating a conversation about CRM because let's face it, the burden will fall on you eventually. You have the opportunity to have a positive influence now that not only will make your life easier but the lives of everyone with whom you interact to support customers.

SECTION 5

SPEAKING ABOUT RELATIONSHIPS

CRM REQUIRES YOU UNDERSTAND HOW RELATIONSHIPS WORK; IT'S PATTERNS OF ESTABLISHMENT, GROWTH, AND DETERIORATION.

re·la·tion·ship \ noun \-shən-ˌship\: the state of being connected by reason of an established or discoverable quality[11]

"The quality of your life is the quality of your relationships."

- Anthony Robbins

Withdrawing our focus from acronyms and gimmicks, and resolving to collaborate on the CRM effort through open and sincere dialog unites us in building relationships that last. The word "relationship" is not just at the center of the CRM acronym; it is its foundation and purpose. As I collaborate with people to implement the processes and technology that power customer strategies, I am constantly reminded of the customer we serve. I have to be careful not to allow meetings and project deadlines to distract me from what matters. When the going gets tough, it is easy to focus on implementing software, putting people through training, creating business workflows, and marking tasks as "completed." I have to go back to thinking about the customer and the people that come to work every day to be of fervid service to them.

When the focus is on people, those transactional minutes can turn into moments of exuberance and even bliss. Even more so when your products and services have a profound impact on the lives of people (even humanity as a whole). Many of you have seen CRM improve processes that help a company cut operational costs and gain market share, but have you seen it change lives? Sometimes (not often enough) CRM is about helping people meet the most fundamental needs for healthcare and human services. It is true that sometimes CRM is just a tool to manage your pipeline. But for many people, your "customer" is a patient; a child whose life you will enrich by improving childcare services systems in their state. Or a single mother who will be able to spend a little extra quality time with her children on her way to her third job because someone was mindful of her needs. Or a hospice caregiver now able to help people more efficiently.

The common theme in what CRM does for every organization is that it helps your company focus on people. Both for the companies changing the world, and the companies making customers happy one at a time, CRM is about building and nurturing relationships. For companies swallowed up in CRM technical practices driven strictly by numbers and analytics, this can be a difficult mental transition to make. To them, "relationship" has to do only with the way relational databases maintain links between customer records. For CRM to achieve its true purpose, "relationship" must be about the way people connect. This is where the rubber meets the road with CRM. If customer relationship strategies are not about "relationships" and the activities and interactions that forge human relationships, then all you are doing is collecting names of people that will eventually go buy from your competitor. Relationships are not about databases or impersonal transactions; they are about people. The fact that they are "business" relationships does not change how relationships work.

Tim Sanders, former Chief Solution Officer at Yahoo, brought this to light in his book "Love Is the Killer App."[12] Tim uses terms like "love-cat" to describe people whose willingness to share information and insight are based on generosity and genuine desire to help others through relationships that are more meaningful. The book is filled with concepts that, like the word relationship, sometimes make business people uncomfortable: terms like giving, generosity, sharing, compassion and even love. The business climate is changing to become more receptive to the idea that we are building "personal" relationships through processes compatible with the ways we build personal relationships outside of work. Extrication of the word "relationship" from the terms "customer" or "client" or "employee" or "partner" is like removing its soul.

Unfortunately, you face the reality of a workplace where CRM is about "technology" rather than "people" and the processes that help you gain their loyalty. Technology companies have driven what CRM is and what it means for far too long. We have allowed it in exchange for quick fixes that result in costly implementations. We opt to implement tools that, while very cool, were never intended to replace your efforts to cultivate relationships. They were intended to create more time for you to be of even greater service to customers. Cultivating relationships, you see, requires labor, care, and even study. CRM tools were meant to give us more time to listen to customers, improve their experiences, make them feel good about how well we addressed their expectations.

THE A, B, C's... AND D AND E OF RELATIONSHIPS

Relationship building is decisive. It prompts us to ask questions like, "With whom do I want to build a meaningful relationship?" and "What interactions lead to a stronger relationship?" Interpersonal relationships are interesting to study, to say the least, and there are people who dedicate their life to analyzing how we establish both the brief and enduring relationships in our personal and business lives. This chapter is not an in-depth study of human psychology, but it does compel you to think about the nature of relationships and the similarities between how we establish them, nourish them, and even end them.

What if I told you that in my twenty-four years of marriage, neither my wife Shelley nor I have ever done anything meaningful or intentional to keep our relationship healthy? Or that we simply met one day and, without any formulated ideas about what we wanted in a relationship decided to get married? And that every day over the last twenty-four years we have made no conscious effort to solve problems or evaluate risks or ponder on the value of the relationship? Would you believe me? Would you in the least suspect that there was something strange about the relationship if I asserted that no effort was ever put into it since we said, "I do," yet it was thriving? What if I added that through happy times, hardships, difficulties, and five children together, we never made any investments into the relationship after reciting our marriage vows? Surely, you would wonder if I am telling you the whole story.

The truth is that I knew the qualities I wanted in a mate ever since I was a teenager (so did my wife …and lucky me, I was a close match). That is the case with most people who want to have a meaningful relationship. You know what you want from a relationship. The more significant the relationship, the more time you spend listening, reading and asking people about how to improve it. As a father of five and grandfather of two, I give a lot of thought to how much time I should spend with each child, always mindful that they all have different needs and expectations. Developing and retaining relationships takes special care and attention. They get better when we pay attention to them, and they deteriorate when we do not.

Why then, would you expect to have a good relationship with customers without doing anything to understand how they prefer to do business with you, or if they consider their experiences with you worthy of sharing with others? Why is it so common for companies to sell a product to a customer with such fervor, but then not speak to them again unless they are trying to upsell them? Business relationships follow similar (often identical) patterns of formation and growth as personal relations. Technology (CRM or otherwise) can't correct bad behavior without an intentional customer relationship strategy that helps define the relationships your business should nurture. Without relationship strategies technology could potentially keep you busy focusing on the relationships that will drain your resources and budget. We build processes for sending customers information, tracking their issues, managing their data, and tracking their orders, but too often overlook that relationships have a process that we should manage with equal skill.

In their book, "Close Relationships: Perspectives on the Meaning of Intimacy,"[13] George Levinger and Harold L. Raush explain that personal relationships can go through stages and follow natural processes towards growth or deterioration. They explain how relationships, which begin with mutual attraction or interest, display some predictable patterns. Using the ABCDE mnemonic, Levinger and Raush explain in a theoretical, but logical, manner the phases relationships go through.

- In the "acquaintance" stage, a couple may be in contact purely because of a mutual attraction or interest.

- In the "build-up" phase, parties engage in self-disclosure and become increasingly interdependent.

- In the "continuation" stage, lives become enmeshed and the relationship becomes consolidated.

- In the "deterioration" phase, the relationship may deteriorate due to an imbalance of costs and rewards, or a high number of risk factors.

- In the "end" stage, the relationship reaches deterioration that may lead the parties to end the relationship.

We know that there is a marked difference between business and personal relationships. We define a business relationship as "an association between individuals or companies entered into for commercial purposes and sometimes formalized with legal contracts or agreements."[14] We say business relationships bind us only through the contracts we forge with one another. Personal relationships are bound similarly by covenants we make with one another. Both personal and business relationships are based on trust. You cultivate both through transparent and mutual accountability. Either can deteriorate when we do not keep our agreements. So, while the nature of the agreements we make with one another in personal and business relationships differs, how we build relationships is very similar. In fact, business relationships follow a pattern almost identical to the personal relationship stages presented by Levinger and Raush.

Given the similarities between the way interpersonal and business relationships emerge, it is no surprise that generational differences are influencing what we call a "relationship" and how we go about managing it. Some companies make the mistake of seeing cultural changes and the way new generations build relationships as the "end of relationship sales." I have even heard some customer strategist say that the new generation of buyers does not see doing business as a "relationship" anymore.

It is true that culture has changed immensely in the past twenty years. Western culture is more relaxed about what a relationship is. What we called "traditional courtship," where the families of the dating couple have an active part in the courtship itself, is not as common. Similarly, businesses use to follow a linear process of identifying potential customers, bringing them into their customer relationship management process, and transitioning them methodically through linear sales process phases. We see these phases, still, deeply embedded into many CRM tools. So yes, I agree that the world is changing and that businesses need to change with the times and become supportive of the way people buy. The lifestyle of the new generation of customers influences their expectations across personal and business interactions. People meet online and fall in love without ever meeting in person. People learn about you and buy your products without ever speaking to someone in your company. HOWEVER, the lack of face-to-face interaction does not change the fact that this is still a relationship, albeit of a less traditional type. What has changed is that people in both personal and business life are leveraging technology (greatly influenced by social and generational influences) to define how they want to engage. They expect you to figure out where and how proactively.

You have to start looking at your business relationships as relationships; not connections or sales or contacts. You have to engage at the relationship level because it is the best way to manage the interactions and experiences that create emotional connections (what we now know truly keeps customers coming back). When you engage from the "relationship," you are better prepared to address the issues more important to that stage of the relationship and can influence the outcome. Like in personal relationships, you have to learn what it takes to build a relationship or keep it from deteriorating at "that" stage and within the expectations and agreements of that stage. As a father of five, I have learned that it takes a lot of work to understand kids. I have read dozens of books on parenting and have even attended a course or two on being a better parent. That is because the parent-child relationship has specific nuances and expectations, which vary depending on the stage of the relationship. Your relationships with significant others (platonic and romantic), your relationships with parents, siblings, and friends all require similar focus and skill. So do customer relationships, and it is time we begin seeing them as what they are and learn skillfully to manage them.

Business relationships have various stages that CRM strategies and CRM tools must manage:

ACQUAINTANCE PHASE: LEADING WITH LEADS

We replace the "acquaintance" phase with words such as "suspect, prospect, and lead." In this stage, the relationship is dependent on things like previous direct or indirect contact or mutual needs and interests. Leads often become business prospects or business connections we leverage to win or keep customers. Leads can become references, mouthpieces with whom you maintain an indefinite acquaintance relationship. Leads can progress to become customers, partners, or employees. However, the truth about why we identify someone as a "lead" (let's be honest) is that we want it to "lead" somewhere (thus the term). Saying that we are only interested in meeting someone to see where it "leads" may sound a bit shallow, but it is the reality of why we meet people (in personal and business life). We are all investing time and money to serve customers, employees and partners better. This is the most important first step in relationship building: investing in the right relationships.

In other words, you and your company must decide in which relationships to invest. You are assessing not only which relationships present an opportunity to close a sale, but to which relationships you will commit and on which you will invest. I come from a very conservative background in which boys are expected to court girls before considering marriage. My dad was adamant about me only dating girls I would consider marrying. As I got older, I deviated (significantly) from that goal and learned from experience how brilliant his advice really was. It is exhausting to spend so much emotional capital in a relationship that leads nowhere. Lead qualification is the speed-date of the business world. This is the step where you quantify the type of relationship it will become and the level of investment you are going to make to pursue, maintain, or end it.

You may find comparing leads to a potential romantic partner humorous, but Tom Searcy, author of "RFPs Suck! How to Master the RFP System Once and for All"[15] suggests that:

"When a prospect calls, your objective should be to start dancing and see if it leads to romance."

Courtship is expensive, and when you are running a business, you have to spend wisely and evaluate the potential a relationship has for success. Companies with strict policies that require salespeople to present their case and show evidence that there is a real opportunity before approving a "pursuit" budget (discretionary funds to pursue a relationship) are wise. Many of these policies also help salespeople with damage control, ensuring you leave a positive impression even if it is not a relationship you want to pursue. We live in an era where social media is both generous and unforgiving. It gets the word out about the positive things you do and spreads like wildfire when you mistreat people. As with dating, it is hard to find the love of your life when everyone you have ever dated thinks you are a jerk. CRM applications provide a great advantage in this area by allowing you to keep lead information segregated from active sales activity, while still connecting to the interactions you have with non-customers. CRM system features that link relationship types are extremely useful. They help you discover the connections that exist between people so you can leverage them to sell products, build stronger connections, and even restore relationships.

SELF-DISCLOSURE PHASE: THE NEED FOR TRANSPARENCY

As with personal relationships, business relationships grow when we are open and transparent with customers and create an environment that promotes and earns transparency. Trust opens revolving doors for self-disclosure, which must be a primary goal in any CRM process. The need for transparency and self-disclosure and business relationships that become increasingly interdependent is indispensable. Dennis DeGregor, author of "The Customer-Transparent Enterprise," poses this question as he elaborates on the need for customer transparency:

"The development of the Customer-Transparent business model came about from asking ourselves the following question: In a rapidly changing 21st century technology environment, where the customer has 24x7x365 access to information and SS&M processes through an ever-increasing array of distribution channels, and where the customer increasingly 'sell themselves' and demands a self-designed experience, what is the impact of this evolving customer behavior on corporate productivity?" [16]

Transparency and self-disclosure are important because they allow us to go directly to the need and openly discuss ways to meet it through mutual self-disclosure and collaboration. Because CRM manages more than relationships with customers, consider the following benefits of transparency and self-disclosure across all of your business relationships:

• With customer and partner relationships: Facilitates strategic and solution-driven conversations that result in real value to your business.

• Within customer interactions: Enables you to explore better ways to serve and correct mistakes of the past.

• Within employee relationships: Transparency and self-disclosure allow you to share the company-wide vision and win the commitment of people as contributors and champions. It also allows you to listen to honest feedback about the way current initiatives are affecting people personally and professionally. Remember, you have to take care of the people who are rewarding the customer for doing business with you.

CRM is, once again a great vehicle for driving the businesses processes that promote and solicit transparency from your customers, but it must integrate with all the efforts that collect honest customer feedback. Feedback cannot be limited to the perception of the people interacting with customers, who simply ask in general terms how the interaction went. Lack of granularity in asking questions yields shallow feedback. There are some great instruments you should incorporate into CRM tools to gain a balanced perspective of customer sentiment. Net Promoter Scores (NPS), for example can help you determine which customers are promoting your products and services. Cx Index measurements are also a great source of information. So are customer surveys (word of mouth, voice of the employee, voice of the customer, etc.). The goal is to get as much transparent feedback and self-disclosure from customers as possible, and use that feedback to become more transparent yourself.

During a conversation with a friend who leads the customer experience efforts at a multi-billion dollar US company I asked, "Do you feel that you are transparent with your customers?" She struggled with the response. After a few moments, she said something that cuts to the heart of what transparency is. She said, "I think we give them a transparent experience across our brands. The sales and service experience feels the same across all our channels. But if by 'transparency' you mean openness, communication, and accountability, then we are doing a very poor job." She nailed it! Transparency is about more than truth in advertisement or information sharing with customers. It is about more than giving them the technology that moves them "transparently" from one technology to the next without experiencing a different interface or brand across your many sub-brands. Transparency is about openness, communication, and accountability. When your customers feel you are not open to deal with problems, honest in your communications, and accountable for your actions, they will perceive the relationship as risky or as having an imbalance of risks versus rewards. Incidentally, this is a rule that applies to customers as well and a consideration for terminating the customer relationship. A company cannot continue to make investments in a customer who is not committed to openness, communication, and accountability.

CONSOLIDATION PHASE: GETTING SERIOUS

Customers do not make a decision to formalize their relationship with you through a purchase or contract until they get to the phase in the relationship where they can trust you. The consolidation phase is only a point in time that also represents a continuous commitment to the relationship. It does not mean that you don't have to work to maintain that commitment you worked so hard to achieve through transparency. This is the stage in the customer relationship where you can make plans for the future and where you can start acting like a there is a mutual investment and future. Yes, future... I know that some of you will push back at the idea of long-term relationships with customers, referencing the many times you buy items on Amazon only once. However, although it is true that I may never buy another Proctor-Silex 33043 4-Quart Slow Cooker (a gift for my daughter-in-law) or another Amopé Pedi Perfect Electronic Pedicure Foot File (I refuse to reveal who it was for), I do intend to buy again from Amazon. Although I may not see a long term relationship with either one of the suppliers, there is potential for them to have a long-term customer relationship with me through another product or service they provide.

You should aim to reach this stage as a natural result of building relationships based on self-disclosure and transparency. Here relationships become more consolidated and open. Anyone who has been in a relationship for a long time knows the importance of this stage. In this stage, if the customer sees the grass greener on your competitor's yard, then it is time for you to water your lawn and probably paint your fence. The continuation stage is where we get to balance the perception of costs and rewards and can reduce risks to the relationship. Here is where we show people that we are not only interested in winning them but keeping them and rewarding them for their commitment to the relationship. As with personal relationships, business relationships require you make the necessary investments to keep people aware of the value you offer them, and the things you do to manage relationship risks.

DETERIORATION PHASE: PREVENTING THE END

Not all relationships deteriorate, but when they do, there are always signs that the relationship was in trouble. Sadly, over-dependence on technology to remind you of when you should be talking to a customer can keep you from seeing the relationship deteriorate as it happens. Salespeople experience this when they wait for an automated email to remind them that a customer's yearly maintenance is due, only to call the customer and realize, to their embarrassment, the customer is about to leave him for a competitor.

Dissatisfaction and resentment are not reserved for personal relationships. They happen in business and cause people to communicate less and avoid self-disclosure. They also cause people to lose trust in you and your company and ultimately send the relationship into a sometimes-irreparable state that leads to the end of the relationship. Fortunately for your company, the single most important cause of deterioration is preventable. By constantly accessing the balance of risk and rewards and how customers perceive you as providing value and lowering risks, you can prevent customer relationship deterioration.

ENDING PHASE: A PREVENTABLE STAGE

Business relationships can end with as much heartache and drama as a personal relationship. Both can result in hurt feelings and a range of emotions (from relief to anger). When business relationships end because both parties understand that they are better apart than together, the breakup can be easier to accept. When business relationships meet a bitter end, the damage, both emotional and financial, can be as bad as a divorce. In cases where it is you or your company that has violated the customer's trust, the following advice from the Mayo Clinic on mending a broken marriage is applicable, sobering, and worth incorporating into the CRM practices of your organization:

- BE ACCOUNTABLE. Take responsibility for your actions. End the behavior that caused the loss of trust immediately. Be honest. Once the initial shock is over, discuss what happened openly and honestly — no matter how difficult talking or hearing about the problem may be.

- CONSIDER SHARED GOALS. It may take time to sort out what has happened and to consider whether your relationship can heal. If you share a goal of reconciliation, realize that recovering trust will take time, energy, and commitment.

- CONSULT A THIRD PARTY trained in the issue that caused the problem. Third parties such as conflict mediators can help you put the situation in perspective, identify issues that may have contributed to it, help you learn how to rebuild and strengthen the relationship, and avoid ending it.

- MAKE EVERY EFFORT TO RESTORE TRUST at any cost, even if the relationship will end or has ended anyway.

DISPELLING RELATIONSHIP MYTHS

As with personal relationships outside of work, there are many myths and misunderstandings about what it takes to maintain a relationship healthy and growing. We bring some of these myths with us to the workplace and subsequently incorporate them into our business processes. Most common among them are the following misconceptions about relationship building:

- Relationships that appear to be healthy do not require work. You have heard the expression that relationships are like gardens that need care and cultivation to stay healthy. This analogy is as true about customer relationships as it is about personal relationships. Strong, enduring relationships between people require proactive focus.

- If you have a good relationship, you should be able to anticipate what the other person needs and feels. This one is tricky. While it is true that the better you know a person or company, the better and more proactively you will be able to provide for their needs, you have to be careful to base your efforts on facts. If you do not think consumers expect you to be proactive in knowing what they need, take note of the relationship Apple has with their MacHeads, or Dunkin Donuts with their fans. Both groups look with anticipation for these companies to understand them and anticipate their needs. CRM strategies require that you take into account the feelings and expectations people have about you and the feelings and expectations they communicate to you and one another. This one is true.

- Conflict ruins relationships. Companies avoid conflict with customers and, in the process, miss the opportunity to resolve problems. Conflicts do not ruin relationships. Failure to resolve conflict ruins relationships.

- In order for a relationship to be successful, the other person must change. At first glance this statement seems to agree with the "customer is always right" attitude championed by Harry Gordon Selfridge (1857-1947) founder of London's Selfridges department store. What he (and other 20th-century companies like Marshall Field's) were trying to institute was the idea that we should treat the customer as if they were right, even when they were not. This is a mental attitude that stimulates empathy and opens a dialog that leads to a better understanding of customer needs. The customer already expects you to give them the benefit of the doubt. Therefore, your CRM business processes must align with this mindset.

Like with all human associations, it takes a conscious, concentrated effort to maintain a healthy relationship. The five stages originally proposed by Dr. Levinger are purely theoretical and logical. It is difficult to see when or where one crosses the boundary between one phase and another. Therefore, it is important to emphasize the idea of transitions among the phases. Sometimes acquaintanceships lead to the third phase without progressing through the stages. The model is primarily a rhetorical device and not truly amenable to "research." However, it helps us to visualize how relationships can progress.

Perhaps the most interesting aspect of the similarities between personal and business relationships is that the ultimate decision for continuing or ending is based on an emotional connection.

We are, after all, human beings driven to decisions based on both facts and feelings. Referenced earlier, the Customer Experience Index, identified by Forester Research, clearly credits a customer's willingness to consider you for another purchase, likelihood to recommend you, and the likelihood to switch to a competitor on how they rate their experiences with you. Customers, at each interaction, are measuring the experience to determine if their needs were met, if you made it easy, and if, as a result, they felt good about it. However, while the alignment of customer experience with customer behavior (and its application to customer strategy) is truly brilliant, it is not new. It is also incomplete unless we learn to assess experiences within the framework of the relationship phases it may go through. Experiences are not independent of relationships and vice versa. It is within the relationship framework, the various relationship phases, and the expectations of each stage that people make value assessments (imbalance in cost, rewards, and risk) to either continue or end the relationship. Experiences build relationships, and relationships define the right experiences to deliver.

The quality of your business, like the quality of your life, is measured by the quality of your relationships. Before you create measurement mechanisms and metrics of your sales pipeline, be sure to measure the quality of your relationships. If your CRM strategy (in particular your sales stages) do not acknowledge the various phases of relationship building, you may not be building customer relationships at all.

SECTION 6

SPEAKING ABOUT INTERACTIONS

CRM MANAGES THE CUSTOMER AND EMPLOYEE INTERACTIONS THAT LEAD TO GENUINE CONNECTIONS.

man·age \ verb \'ma-nij\: to handle or direct
with a degree of skill[17]

"Happiness is not something ready made. It comes from your own actions."

- Dalai Lama

Understanding that customer relationships follow the same patterns of growth and deterioration as other relationships compel us to make our interactions with customers, and the experiences that result from them, intentional and meaningful. We are connected to customers in a relationship that, to be successful, must be reciprocal. It must offer a benefit to both parties for the relationship to be equitable. We manage that reciprocal process during each interaction with customers. The idea that we must "manage" our interactions with people has negative connotations for some who associate the word with oppressive practices in the workplace. In spite of that, the word "manage" is the perfect word to use when talking about customer relationship practices. There are many definitions for the word "manage." The most applicable to CRM being this one from the Merriam-Webster dictionary:

"To handle or direct with a degree of skill."

It applies because the "management" aspect of "customer relationship management" is about skillfully handling (requiring capability) and skillfully directing (requiring intentional strategy) how we handle our customer relationships at the interaction level. Interacting with customers (regardless of communication channel) takes skill. It takes skill to identify interactions that need care and cultivate the ones that are going well. It takes skill to build strategies that incorporate client preferences for interacting with you. It takes skills to listen, learn, and act on the interactions people are having on social media, community forums, events, and anywhere they interact with your company, your partners and other customers. It takes skill to create processes that guide interactions in the right direction.

Great customer experiences are the result of objective and persistent alignment between the interaction and the relationship, in perspective with where the relationship is and in support of all the other customer strategies that support the customer. A phone interaction is never "just" a call. That call is part of a relationship journey that started with the identification of the customer as a good fit. It came about because someone at your company established the right engagement channels and even a customized experience for them. It is supported by customer service and support agreements that set guidance for how you treat them and what to do when you don't meet their expectations. It is part of your company's strategy to present a single, transparent brand to your customer. It is one of many steps you take to connect your customer to your company through great customer experiences. What you perceive as just a phone call may connect your company's relationship, engagement, centricity, service, transparency, and experience strategies for that customer.

It is important to recognize that some companies view "customer interaction management" (CIM) as a completely separate competency managed by contact center systems. It is, for some companies, disconnected from the interactions (and activities) that CRM systems manage. Perhaps because many of the channels used to communicate with customers are managed by call center solutions and the responsibility of call center / contact center teams. Customer relationship management strategies help us build a detailed picture of the customer in order to predict their behavior and create tailored experiences. The interactions that call center systems manage and the history of customer interactions managed in CRM systems, together, help us accomplish that goal.

I intentionally use the word "interaction" instead of "engagement" for two reasons.

1. What we manage through customer relationship management is interaction. Our goal is to interact with the customer one-on-one with mutual and reciprocal action or influence. Once we achieve reciprocity in interacting, we aim for it to hold the customer's attention, and motivate participation that leads to a customer relationship. That connection is called engagement. We use interactions to create customer engagement that opens the door to meaningful customer experiences. Many companies never even reach the interaction or engagement stage. They invest all of their time and money on activities (emails, mailers, and such) that never bring the customer to a one-to-one engagement.

2. Not paying attention to what words mean has created much of the disconnection you are experiencing between you customer efforts. Understanding how activities create

interactions that are engaging is very important to the success of customer relationship management. One of the main goals of this book is to compel you to reconsider how you use terms like centricity, engagement, and experience out of context with what they do to build customer relationships.

INTERACTIONS AND THE CUSTOMER EXPERIENCE

Just as CRM initiatives fail because they did not meet the expectations of the people executing the strategy and using the technology, interactions with customers fail to accomplish their intended purpose when you disconnect them from the experience it is intended to create. Relationships are the affiliations, associations, and connections we have with customers. Customer experiences are what customers use to determine if they want that relationship to grow or end. Interactions are the moments of opportunity you use to create positive customer experiences and must be engaging to capture the customer's interest.

For years, Forester Research has been writing "The Business Impact of Customer Experience" report to help maintain focus on the importance of Customer Experience as a unique competency. As part of an online Q4 2013 survey of 7,506 US consumers about their interactions with 154 large US brands in a range of different industries, Forrester found a parallel between how customers rate their experience with a company and their subsequent choices to remain loyal. Forrester uses a measure called the "Customer Experience Index" (CXi) which uses three models to estimate the impact customer experience has on three loyalty measures:

- Willingness to consider the company for another purchase

- Likelihood to switch business, and

- Likelihood to recommend

The study shows that "the strong correlation between CXi and loyalty means that companies with higher CXi scores tend to have more customers who will buy from them again, who won't take their business elsewhere, and who will recommend them to a friend." Managing the customer experience builds customer relationships, but also directly impacts revenue from customers who stay with you and bring in new customers.

Restaurants often tell you that they want you to have an enjoyable "dining experience." That's because you could have just as well gone through the Burger King drive-through or re-heated last night's dinner at home. The "experience" is why you are there. Other companies will aim for you to have a great "shopping experience" or a pleasant "travel experience." Companies that design customer interactions as channels to great customer experiences understand what customer relationship management is about.

It is what marketing firms like J. D. Power rate when awarding a company a "Highest in Customer Satisfaction Award," an accolade companies like GMC promote as a highly ranked customer experience endorsement. This year GMC received the highest numerical score among mass-market brands in the J.D. Power and Associates Customer Satisfaction with Dealer Service (CSI) Study. The results are based on responses from 91,723 owners and lessees of 2008 to 2012 model-year vehicles, measuring 32 auto manufacturers and measures satisfaction among vehicle owners who visit a dealer for service during the first three years of ownership. Proprietary study results are based on experiences and perceptions of owners surveyed from October-December 2012. The J. D. Power website reads:

"Getting the right information depends on asking, listening, and watching. Of course, asking is the easy part, and is what most survey research is designed to do. Nevertheless, it is not enough to just ask what customers think about your brand or how satisfied they are with your products or services. You also need to listen to what they say and watch what they do."

Customer Relationship Management drives the business processes that enable customer interactions as well as the processes that evaluate and survey the quality of customer experiences. To disconnect the interaction from the experience is myopic and the reason so many people think that Customer Experience Management is disconnected from CRM (and that it is a new strategy designed to supersede CRM). Managing customer experience is a logical function of CRM tools and necessary part of any CRM strategy. For the strategy to be effective, you have to make customer interactions intentional and engaging and customer experiences memorable, from the customer's perspective.

INTERACTIONS AT A DISTANCE

For the past few years, I have been fortunate to work from my home office. My wife, who has her own home-based business, works upstairs from our master bedroom while I work from my office in the basement. Our proximity to one another allows us to go to lunch together frequently. When Shelley needs something from me, all she has to do is give a shout and I respond. Occasionally we rely on text messages for communications requiring a quick response, but most of the time we speak face to face. Working from home is great, and I am one of the lucky few who get to do it these days. However, when I travel, Shelley and I have to get creative with how we communicate. Geography, business hours, time zones, and availability of phone reception and internet access dictate the channels we use to stay in contact, solve problems, or share information. When circumstances are ideal, we both have preferred interaction channels depending on where we are and what we are doing. Like with couples who are away from one another for extended periods, (and in particular with long-distance relationships) we learn to communicate with one another in more efficient and accessible ways. If a particular channel is available to one person, the other will wonder why their significant other isn't using it.

As we emphasize that customer relationships are like other human relationships, we begin to see a pattern emerge, especially between customer relationships and long-distance relationships. You could even say that, for the most part, customer relationships ARE long-distance relationships. Except for companies that enjoy frequent face-to-face interactions with customers (retail stores, hotels, restaurants, etc.), most of our interactions with customers are conducted via channels that do not require a person to be physically present. As with the previous analogy about long-distance relationships, customers know what interaction channels are available and expect you to use them to make it easy to interact.

INTERACTIONS AND COMMUNICATION

How people interact with one another has changed over time. When CRM systems first came into the corporate marketplace (and for many years since), they recorded interactions that took place:

• In person

• Via Email

• Via Phone

• Via Mail

As communication technology evolves, we make adjustments to make sure CRM tools record those interactions adequately. Customer interactions can now include interactions that occur via:

• Web portals

• Kiosks

• Mobile devices

• Messaging

• Text or video chat

These days it is as much about leveraging communication channels as it is about when and where. When customer interactions take place via social media, they may be between your customer and someone with whom you are not even connected. Knowing when to interact can be a challenge. Say you are having coffee at your local coffee house and overhear two people talking. From their conversation, you realize that one of them is a customer of your company. The customer is telling his coffee buddy that he recently had a very negative experience with your company and that they were considering purchasing from the competition the next time they needed services. Do you take the opportunity to offer the customer help? Is the customer's expectation that you should jump in to offer assistance since you overheard the need? Or would they find it intrusive that you initiated a conversation at an external forum, even if it is a public place? What if the person was not your customer and you overheard them say that they were in the market for a new vehicle; one that your car dealership sells? Does the message that there is intent to buy, once again delivered in a public forum, make it acceptable to interact with this person?

These scenarios are just as common in the coffee house as they are on social media, and you will have to decide how to manage them. The decision to interact follows the same rules in both environments. Remember what I said about transparency and the openness it creates so you can have frank conversations with customers? It also applies to social media. It applies to all your channels and the interactions that happen through them. The advent of social media does not create a need for a new type of "Social CRM." It simply requires that CRM strategies take into account that there is yet another channel where customer interactions happen and that it requires special methods to manage it well.

INTERACTIONS IN AN OMNI-CHANNEL WORLD

Technology innovation will continue to bring many more channels you will be able to use to communicate with your customers. What is important is that you treat channels as the bridge you are building to help the customer interact with you in engaging ways that lead to greater mutual transparency. Sometimes it is the bridge that guides them to where they need to go to help themselves. Sometimes it is the bridge that brings them to the best place for you to help them. Sometimes it requires that you build a bridge to where they are. The better scenario is that you allow the customer multiple channels to interact with you. The best scenario is that they can transition seamlessly from one channel to another, based on their needs, without feeling that the channels are disconnected or not part of a single experience.

The idea of "multi-channel" speaks to the customer's ability to reach you in many ways (preferably ways you have identified as most beneficial to them). While "omni-channel" refers to the customer's perception of experiencing those channels as a seamless, unified journey between them. Be careful how you use the terms "multi-channel" and "onmi-channel", especially if you think "multi-channel" is something that needs to be replaced by the cooler practice and technology of "omni-channel". Omni-channel simply refers to the experience we want customers to have. You want them to focus on having their needs met and on you making that easy. If that goal requires multiple channels, then that is the right thing to give the customer, as long as they experience a transparent and seamless experience, as they move through those channels.

CRITICAL POINTS OF INTERACTION

During a conference in New York last year I was asked, as part of a panel of customer executives, to help answer the question "What do customers really want?" I believe my response was, "Thank you for asking me a question only more difficult to answer than 'what do women really want?'". After the audience stopped laughing, I continued to explain that, as a young (incredulous) boy, I thought I understood girls my age only to realize the magnificent complexity of the opposite sex. I also thought I understood women as I started dating, and then after I got married; becoming increasingly knowledgeable as I endeavored to have a great relationship with my wife. Then, just as I thought I had it figured out, I had daughters (then a granddaughter). Each of my daughters is different and responds differently to different situations. Their age, environment, emotional state, perceptions, and expectations change the scenario and compel me to make decisions based on many, constantly changing factors affecting the relationship. Some days it feels like there are no consistent patterns of behavior until I stand back and studiously evaluate each interaction. Then I begin to see patterns and what I call "critical points of interaction."

While there are distinct types of interactions that help qualify prospects, sell a product, or follow up on a complaint, there are particular interactions that can make or break a relationship. They are "critical" because they could result in abrupt changes in a relationship and must be managed with the highest sense of urgency. In this context, the definition of "manage" (to handle or direct with a degree of skill) is even more relevant. Managing is about conscious direction. Applied to relationships, "managing" means treating something with care. It is synonymous with the ideas of leading, caring, negotiating, and overseeing. You must manage critical interactions with surgical precision, acknowledging that they are especially significant to the growth or deterioration of your customer relationships. Psychologists tell us that there are times in our personal relationship when a single event can change the direction of the relationship. Among them is the first use of the word "we," the first fight, discussions about the future, and talks about commitment. They are interactions that turn into defining moments. That is what critical interactions are to customer relationships.

In his book "How to Win Customers and Keep Them for Life,"[18] Dr. Michael LeBoeuf encourages us to be mindful of what he calls the "moments of truth," those crucial points of customer contact when you have the opportunity to share your value proposition and show genuine customer care. I would like to draw from his list and isolate the most critical interactions CRM strategies must manage with extra emphasis:

INTERACTIONS WITH ANGRY OR DEFENSIVE PEOPLE

Not to overstate the obvious, but anger and defensiveness are warning bells that alert you that something is amiss in your relationship with someone. The range of emotions anger provokes can stem from a number of issues. Guiding the conversation towards resolution is always important, even if the problem is not your fault. Between the physical reaction that both parties experience, and the behavior they exhibit is the cognitive experience of anger.

Does the customer feel that what happened was wrong, unfair, or undeserved? Why? What were the events that brought it to pass? Armed with these answers you will be better prepared to solve the problem. Of all the things we manage poorly in our customer relationships, anger and defensiveness rank highest. Returning anger and defensiveness with more anger and defensiveness never ends well. Remember, this is about relationship management, so you must engage people with the mindset that you want to help build the relationship (and yes, that takes skill). Deal first with people's feelings, and then help them with the problem that is making them angry.

Build a CRM strategy that gives employees and partners the resources they need to manage this type of interaction effectively. Knowledge is your greatest asset for dealing with angry and defensive people and CRM tools can provide that knowledge. A well-informed person can disarm an angry customer by showing you care enough to leverage history of past interactions to help them. Better yet, you can create a positive customer experience by using knowledge to accelerate the resolution of their problem. To ensure compliance with your company's service level agreements and best practices for problem resolution, embed business processes and workflow into CRM that guides you through these processes.

INTERACTIONS WHERE A SPECIAL REQUEST IS MADE

Special requests are sometimes a manifestation of something missing or incomplete in what you delivered to the customer. Managing interactions that involve a special request can turn crisis into a successful collaboration with people whose expectations you have not met. That is because special request discussions allow us to listen to what customers want in relation to what they got (and that is always a good thing).

CRM interactions, like special requests, are critical because they can branch off into other profitable interactions for your company:

1. SERVICE OPPORTUNITY – We seldom get an opportunity to show people how much we really care about them, but when we respond positively to a need, it shows that we are willing to be flexible.

2. ASSESSMENT OPPORTUNITY – When someone explains a need or special request it opens doors for questions about how you have done the job to date.

3. PROMOTIONAL OPPORTUNITY – One can never underestimate the importance of self-promotion. Most people do not realize the value of the products and services you provide until you tell them. Here is your chance.

4. BUSINESS OPPORTUNITY – It angers me when I am on a project and one of my teammates gets upset because the customer asks for more than what we originally agreed to do for them. A change request or request for customization should never represent an inconvenience. It should represent an opportunity for new and repeat business.

5. COMPETITIVE ADVANTAGE – Needless to say, if you are always willing to cater to the special needs of people, your competition is going to have a hard time catching up.

INTERACTIONS WHERE THE CUSTOMER CAN'T MAKE UP HIS MIND

When people waver between two or more possible courses of action, they need someone to help guide the way. Indecision provides an opportunity to move people through stages in the relationship. In CRM, we identify not only where people are in their relationship with us, but also who can make decisions about strengthening that relationship. Indecision can be a clear sign that you are not talking to the person that can best nurture the relationship.

Indecision may indicate that the individual you identified in your sales cycle as the "decision-maker" may be the wrong person. To a salesperson, this significant mistake could misdirect them to invest valuable time in efforts that do not lead to growing the relationship or closing the sale. It could mean that while your company is talking to the person you think is responsible for choosing you, the right person may be elsewhere talking to your competition.

Indecision is not only bad for you but also bad for your customer. Every minute of indecision could constitute a delay in delivering something of value. This middle-of-the-road behavior could be a cry for help from customers who need you but do not know how to ask. In either case, staying in the middle of the road is never good.

"Indecision is debilitating; it feeds upon itself; it is, one might almost say, habit-forming. Not only that, but it is contagious; it transmits itself to others... business is dependent upon action. It cannot go forward by hesitation. Those in executive positions must fortify themselves with facts and accept responsibility for decisions based upon them. Often greater risk is involved in postponement than in making a wrong decision." - H. A. Hopf

It falls on us sometimes to move people off the road for their own good by recommending options that help manage the relationship and lead it towards a mutually beneficial choice.

INTERACTIONS THAT RAISE OBJECTIONS OR OBSTACLES

It is amazing what people will tell you when you are truly listening. A person will tell you they do not want to buy, and some people will only hear rejection. However, if you are listening, truly listening, you will see obstacles to remove and objections to address instead.

This is another good instance of people opening doors for you to make your case. When people present objections, they are telling you that they do not see the value of what you are selling. No CRM strategy is more effective than a well-prepared, knowledgeable human being who expertly deals with objections. However, CRM tools can serve as a knowledge repository companies can leverage to maintain value proposition information essential to addressing product and service value. Used correctly, a CRM tool (properly positioned by a well-thought-out CRM strategy) can serve as a knowledge resource immediately available during these interactions.

INTERACTIONS THAT REVEAL INTEREST IN BUYING

Interactions where people tell you they want to buy are happy moments in the life of a company. Unfortunately, not everyone who interacts with the customer gets the hint. As the father of five, four who are adults, I have lots of experience with a humorous teenage phenomenon I like to call "romantic cluelessness." Around the time they start showing interest in the opposite sex, and inviting them to dinner at our house, they start to miss the obvious. Once their visitor leaves, I ask them, "How long has that girl (or boy) liked you?" Their reaction is like that of spraying a cat with a water bottle (matching facial expressions and all). Sometimes you get very clear hints that someone likes you and miss it completely.

There are more interactions affecting the way you build relationships with people in business. Delivering bad news, responding to complaints, and delivering information about a product or service a customer got from you are some of them. They all present opportunities to gain trust, and reward people for positive action. But critical interactions, faithfully managed, can save your business.

SECTION 7

SPEAKING ABOUT THE CUSTOMER

CRM IS ABOUT CUSTOMERS. THEY DETERMINE IF CRM EFFORTS ARE SUCCESSFUL, NOT YOU.

ser·vice \ noun \ˈsər-vəs\: contribution to the welfare of others[19]

"Life's most urgent question is: What are you doing for others?"

- Martin Luther King, Jr.

Managing critical interactions is a natural part of building relationships with customers. All relationships require engaging interactions to survive. Any relationship worth keeping requires an emotional investment and that all parties are willing to be vulnerable and exposed to bring issues to resolution. This proposition feels risky to some, but building relationships is about human interaction, and human beings make decisions based on their perception of the value of the relationship, not yours.

Launching a CRM effort intended to help you win and keep customers, and then measuring its success strictly by how much you think the customer likes you and your company, is myopic and narrow-minded. That's because the only person that matters when it comes to rating the strength of the customer relationship is the customer. We are all faithful servants of the customers we serve, and servants do not give themselves rate cards for their performance. After your teams commit to collaborate in the grand effort we call CRM and agree to focus on relationship building, the only way to measure if you were successful is for your customers to say so.

This is why the CRM industry has such a bad reputation. We formulate strategies and purchase expensive tools to deploy them, but we neglect to evaluate if any of that investment improved the customer's experience and customer's perception of our efforts to serve them. This is an idea fully explored by Peter Hernon and Danuta Nitecki in their study of service quality, "Service Quality:

A Concept Not Fully Explored," at Texas A&M University. The researchers noted that most businesses have an externally imposed requirement to implement service quality principles; an imposition made by customers who expect them to be accountable and compete for their loyalty. Customers who share information about their expectations offer an opportunity for the company to establish a closer personal contact with them. The study asserts, "Fundamental to service quality is the need for cyclic review of service goals and objectives in relation to customer expectations."

WHAT CUSTOMERS NEED FROM YOU

The customer experience is always directly influenced by the quality of your service. And service quality has, for a long time, been defined from at least four perspectives:[20] Excellence, Value, Conformance, and Meeting / Exceeding Expectations. The problem with this model is that:

- EXCELLENCE - Excellence is often externally defined. It may be a worthy aim but one that changes dramatically and rapidly from person to person.

- VALUE - It incorporates multiple attributes, but quality and value are different concepts. One is the perception of meeting or exceeding expectations, and the other stresses benefit to the recipient.

- CONFORMANCE - It facilitates precise measurement,

but users of a service may not know or care about internal specifications.

• MEETING OR EXCEEDING EXPECTATIONS - This definition is all-encompassing and applies across service industries, but expectations change and may be shaped by experiences with other service providers.

According to the study, what customers are looking for is, in fact, simple: they are looking for a confirmation or disconfirmation of their perceptions. Customers rate this perception on five interrelated dimensions that they most value when they evaluate service quality:

1. TANGIBLES - The appearance of physical facilities, equipment, personnel, and communication material.

2. RELIABILITY – The ability to perform the promised service dependably and accurately.

3. RESPONSIVENESS – The willingness to help customers and provide prompt service.

4. EMPATHY - The caring, individualized attention that a firm provides its customers.

5. ASSURANCE – The knowledge and courtesy of employees and their ability to inspire trust and confidence.

Any strategy or technology that aims to manage customer relationships at any level must incorporate mechanisms that track against these traits and uses them as a baseline to improve the customer experience. A more important question than how a business process will be implemented or automated is "Did it increase the perception of empathy with the customer?" A better measure of the success of a newly implemented service level agreement is "Did it improve responsiveness to customer needs?"

These are qualities all members of your organization must emulate across sales, marketing, support, service, supply chain, and advocacy programs. It must happen at all levels of your company (not just by management or customer-facing functions) through behavior, the customer will "feel" and experience. You need sales and opportunity pipeline management, marketing campaign response tracking, service level maintainability, and other operational components that measure the financial health and revenue pipeline of your business. But what wins and keeps customers is service that improves the customer experience. In asking the following questions, you ensure that every interaction leads to the correct experience for the customer:

IS YOUR SERVICE TANGIBLE?

Companies do not spend millions of dollars on advertising during the Super Bowl to be funny; they do so to be memorable. Advertisement is designed to present a certain image that draws the customer's attention. That attention is going to engender a response.

Anything the customer sees, feels, touches, hears, or smells concerning you and your company is shaping their perception of service quality. Restaurants understand this well. The slightest negative perception that an establishment is dirty could close a restaurant. That is why even when a health department favorably grades a restaurant it can still lose business if its patrons even perceive it to be unclean. Appearances can be deceiving, but customers draw many conclusions about how much you value them from what they see.

Besides using their four senses, customers have a talent for identifying when something is wrong with a company. They may not be able to verbalize it sometimes, but they know. Real service has to be precisely identified. When your service is forced or insincere customers know it. Tangible service is something customers will experience with their senses and also identify by the integrity and authenticity they perceive in your service quality.

IS YOUR SERVICE RELIABLE?

Do people feel that you and your company can be trusted? People want you to be predictable in your patterns of behavior as much as they want to depend on you to do what you say you are going to do. People want consistent performance out of your interactions. If you want to know if you are reliable, then the following statements must be true:

- I do what I say I will do.

- I do it when I say I will do it.

- I aim to do it right the first time.

- I get it done on time.

Reliability is about the consistent behavior that makes you credible in the eyes of people. Credibility is the measure of trust. When people see you as credible, they are willing to give you their trust on credit. Strong relationships require peace of mind and credibility gives people security, integrity, and the assurance that they can trust you even if someone else in the same role or position failed them. Credibility is your door to second chances, a benefit that businesses need to stay competitive.

IS YOUR SERVICE RESPONSIVE?

Being responsive means being accessible, available, and willing to help, which can translate to the time it took to respond as much as to the nature and temperament of the response. By definition, being responsive means, "responding especially, readily and sympathetically to appeals, efforts, and influences."

It is particularly applicable to CRM, which tries to appeal to specific audiences in an effort to influence their decisions through relationship building. CRM strategies and technology don't just account for service response time and expediency. They also track responsiveness, which helps you:

• Create realistic service level agreements

• Build automated processes that help people improve response time

• Measure the efforts that lead to customer satisfaction and peer collaboration

IS YOUR SERVICE EMPATHETIC?

What better use of CRM than to understand more clearly if you and your company have the right measure of empathy as perceived by customers. When you are empathetic, you are experiencing the feelings, thoughts, and attitudes of another. CRM strategies must enable you to understand people better in order to treat them as unique individuals, with their unique personalities and distinctive wants and reasoning, so you can create unique experiences for them. When we look beyond our own needs to understand the needs of others, we experience empathy. When we imagine their problems and walk through them in our minds to help resolve them, we experience empathy. We can express empathy sometimes without saying a word. And because our goal is to build genuine relationships with people, sometimes that conscious empathy turns into sincere sympathy for people that motivates us to understand their distress and help alleviate it. At that moment, we come to the transcendent understanding that compassion is not reserved for our personal relationships.

DOES YOUR SERVICE INSPIRE TRUST?

A customer's perception of service through their assessment of how reliable, responsive, and empathetic you are, is helping them build an inevitable conclusion about your trustworthiness. Trust may be the single most important ingredient in the development and growth of any relationship. Several major theories, including attachment theory (Bowlby, 1969) and Erikson's (1963) theory of psychosocial development, are built on the premise that higher levels of trust in relationships early in life lay the psychological foundation for happier and better functioning relationships in adulthood. It is, therefore, reasonable to expect that customers are happier when you build a foundation for mutual trust.

Customers watch your behavior and ask, although not usually aloud: "Can I trust this person? Can I trust this company?" They want the assurance that they can put their confidence in you and rely on your honesty, dependability, and strength of character. They want to know that you do not have to be coerced or compelled to keep your word. Customers want to have faith in your ability or word in those specific areas where you provide them service.

Remember that Customer Experience as a measurement of customer retention and referral asks customers about functionality and accessibility. It encourages you to ask if your interactions with customers created value by providing the customer what they needed, making it easy to interact with you, and building emotional connections to your company and brand. You can't ask the functionality, accessibility, and emotion questions if bad service is a barrier to providing any of these things. You build relationships by building trust and ensuring transparency through every interaction, always conscious of the service qualities customers expect from you. These behaviors and the unification of the customer strategies that manage them leads to customer experience that keeps customers and motivate them to recommend you to others.

More than technology you need business processes to help you set the correct expectations and sense of value for customers. Creating strategies that manage engagement, centricity, service, support and transparency will help you deliver a great customer experiences. Together, your customer relationship strategies help you give customers accessibility, functionality, and emotional connection that also helps your employees and partners feel rewarded for being part of the customer effort.

However, technology can serve as a tool to give you more time and better insight to make your customer relationship effort for genuine and effective. That is the topic of the next section of this book.

PART TWO

SECTION 8

SPEAKING ABOUT CRM TOOLS

CRM TOOLS ARE ENABLERS. THEY HELP YOU MANAGE CUSTOMER RELATIONSHIPS WITH GREATER EFFICIENCY.

```
in·stru·ment \ noun \'in(t)-strə-mənt\:
a means whereby something is achieved,
performed, or furthered²¹
```

"Technology is nothing. What's important is that you have a faith in people, that they're basically good and smart, and if you give them tools, they'll do wonderful things with them."

- Steve Jobs

In the 1999 science-fiction movie "Bicentennial Man," Robin Williams stars as Andrew, an android who, through his interactions with his human owners and the world around him, endeavors to become human himself. In his role as a computerized servant, Andrew struggles to understand the idiosyncrasies of his biological masters though sometimes humorous but always touching moments. Andrew's mission in life is service. He ends every interaction by saying, "One is glad to be of service"; an automatic, meaningless response built into his subroutines. Gradually, Andrew acquires emotions and realizes the importance of relationships and heartfelt service to others. He makes his trademark phrase his purpose in life.

Until technology makes it possible for a machine to assess the relationships most profitable to your business and create engaging interactions and empathetic service that leads to great customer experiences, you are on your own. Technology cannot create the type of connection required for real relationships. However, it CAN facilitate the communications necessary for that bond to strengthen. It can serve as an enabling, powerful tool for the people tasked with building customer relationships. That is what CRM tools and applications do: they enable you to spend less time on the mundane and more time on your relationships.

The best-known and most widely used CRM tools can give you a 360-degree view of your customer's data. Used correctly and with the collaboration of its users, CRM can give you a valuable

360-degree view of your relationship with customers as well. The first use is purely transactional and leverages the "relational" nature of the software. The second leverages the practices we have discussed in this book to make CRM about building "relationships" that last. Not just relationships with customers, but also with the employees and partners that serve them. CRM that is purely about contact record management, report generation, and other purely transactional activities, removes the "relationship" at the center of CRM.

CRM technology has evolved from a contact-centric (Rolodex-type) system to more advanced relational database systems able to connect contacts to the companies with whom they are associated (as well as to the various sales opportunities, invoices and service tickets related to that contact). Even though not all CRM strategies require that you implement CRM technology, there are many valuable advantages to doing so:

• CRM technology is organized around the contact / account-centric model instead of products or territories. Most relational CRM applications are built on an account-centric model that allows you to see companies and contacts in relationship to one another while extending your visibility into the products and services you offer them within a geographical area or territory. The "customer" (client, citizen, constituent, or patient) remains at the center, with peripheral relationships to the people with whom they interact both inside and outside of your company.

• CRM technology allows you to learn who your most profitable customers are. This practice is significant because, in most markets, 80 percent or more of the profits come from 20 percent or less of the customers. Being able to identify top customers (and what makes them so) will make you more cognizant of the patterns that create new ones just like them. CRM applications include dashboards and list management tools that can leverage existing data to identify the very important and valuable 20 percent and the people who are nurturing those relationships.

• CRM is becoming more like people: Social. The CRM software industry is slowly moving away from mass marketing functions and is leveraging live customer intelligence (LCI) and social engagement to help CRM users target the audience they want to reach. This activity used to be unidirectional (from companies to the consumer). New technology now also allows us to listen, understand, and act on what the customer really wants.

• CRM incorporates employee management tools to help you hire, train, motivate, and keep employees who take special care of the customer. Although the core functionality of CRM applications is customer-centric, it also has a foundation for the more holistic approach of maintaining all relationship data in the same system. CRM allows you to track the interaction between employee and customer, identify patterns of behavior that led to customer acquisition and retention, and even allows you to map the level and depth of relationship between the two.

- CRM manages interactions and activity history efficiently. The ability to document feedback gained through the type of discovery and self-disclosure this book promotes is invaluable.

- CRM technology, using activity and process automation, can remind you to engage in the interactions that cultivate relationships.

- CRM solutions include "Neglected Contacts" reports (a perfect name for what we often do to the people we call "valued customers"), and analytics that give you diagnostic, descriptive, predictive, and prescriptive insight about customers.

INVESTING IN THE RIGHT THING

While these are all compelling reasons to invest in and use CRM technology, not every company buys a CRM tool for the right reasons. In a May 2009 article, MSN Money's Michael Brush recounts a 2007 NPR interview with former Federal Reserve chairperson Alan Greenspan. Among the items offered by

Greenspan was the suggestion that we need to look no further than our underwear drawer as an indicator of financial health. Both Brush and Greenspan argue that the proverbial and literal underwear drawer hold the key to our spending patterns. Economists agree that the sale of underwear raises and falls with the economy. Why knickers? Because they are representative of a much hidden and intimate choice we make when things get tough. As Greenspan also says, "underwear is something we can hold off on buying until we really have the money."

Female readers will note, on the other hand, that women have a completely different perspective on purchasing undergarments. Most women will purchase lingerie because of the way the purchase will make them feel. Feeling stressed and want to reward yourself with something intimate and special? Buy some lingerie.

What an interesting coincidence? Our two most common reasons for buying CRM solutions resemble our reasoning for buying underwear. You wait to invest in the technology customers can't see until things are better financially. Or you buy it to feel good that, even if you don't have a strategy to implement it, you are at least doing something about the CRM need. Then there are those who justify their CRM technology purchase solely on hype. These are the companies that go to trade shows and listen to technology companies explain what CRM "can do" rather than what it "needs to do" or what customers need it to do. These are all bad reasons to implement CRM technology.

Yes, being able to connect with contacts via social media-enabled CRM tools can help you support and sell to more customers. However, how are you leveraging this capability to build the right relationships and improve the experiences of your customers? Access to customer data from mobile devices is now easier than ever through cloud-enabled onboard technology in planes. But what is the best way for flight attendants to use it to improve the customer experience? Can the attendant leverage it to view a passenger's travel history so she can proactively give them the best possible experience, thank them for their patronage, or rectify poor service from a previous flight? Would it negatively affect operational efficiency in-flight or improve it? How does mobile access to information help build, maintain, or restore relationships? If I had a bad experience during my flight from Atlanta to LA and the flight attendant on the connecting flight from LA to Sydney offers me a complimentary drink for my trouble from the previous flight, would I say she was being responsive or intrusive? Would I post it as a negative or positive experience on Facebook where other potential customers can see it?

What if you walked into a retail store? The sales associate (having access to your shopping history from his Google Glass device) asked you if you would be interested in a tie to match the suit you bought the previous week? Would you find that incredibly responsive or would you find it creepy and never buy at that store again? How would immediate access to data affect your relationship with the customer? I am not trying to discount the value of social, mobility, and cloud technology to make CRM better. I am simply motivating you to evaluate if you are using technology to improve the customer experience or if you are just trying to keep up with the Joneses.

Still open for your consideration is that no single CRM application has all the answers. Success in any initiative must include a strong, documented, and tested understanding of the business processes and practices that make your company successful, independent from the technology. CRM strategy and technology go hand-in-hand. If you commit to nurturing your relationships and manage the right interactions, you will be successful in both CRM strategy and technology deployment. A number of factors will skew or sharpen your perception of what CRM technology is and how it applies to your company. Before you dismiss CRM technology based on what you read online or hear from the IT community, take the time to evaluate and research the facts. Have an open mind and exercise fair judgment of what your company is doing with it.

The 2006 Forrester study, referenced in Section 3, is still as timely as ever and discusses best practices for ensuring the successful implementation of CRM solutions. These include:

- Defining data requirements and data quality approach early

- Fostering user adoption

- Placing a high priority on software usability

- Simplifying the CRM platform

- Actively managing the CRM vendor/partner relationship

The good news about making the right choices with CRM technology is that we are the fortunate recipients of the gift of the internet and its unlimited access to feedback from people willing to give it. Type (or speak) a search like "CRM challenges in the retail industry" into a search engine and you gain immediate access to the thoughts of millions of people. Use that information to understand the value of CRM tools and what it will take for your company to make CRM technology implementation a success.

PAYING ATTENTION TO CHANGE

Chinese philosopher Lao Tzu said, "If you do not change direction, you may end up where you are heading." This is advice fitting to the state of CRM technology and the need to change how we manage customer relationship communications and experiences. Industry researchers are using terms like "imminent" and "disruptive" to describe the technologies that are changing CRM application and use. Imminent, because many of these changes are looming close by and are unstoppable stages in our technology evolution. Disruptive, because many of these changes are already here and forcing you to make business investments necessary to stay competitive. These technologies also disrupt the linear processes we have used for years to manage sales, marketing, and service interactions. They allow the customer to learn about you, make purchase decisions, get help, compare options, and buy on their terms and outside what we once knew as the linear customer lifecycle. In the new customer lifecycle, the experience does not begin when the customer buys. It happens every time the customer has a need and technology allows them to begin that cycle in many more places, with a lot more tools. Social and cultural changes in our customer's lives are forcing us to keep up.

When Gartner analysts delivered their keynote "The Nexus of Forces Changes Everything" at the Gartner Symposium/ITxpo 2012, it stimulated us to acknowledge collectively that we had to make significant changes to the current state of CRM technology. Search the acronym "CRM" online and you will find dozens of articles on how innovations in social media, the acceptance of cloud hosting, the dependency and commonplace use of mobile devices and the ability to interpret and use data is changing our world. Gartner calls these "converging and mutually reinforcing social, cultural, and technological factors" the "Nexus of Forces." IDC calls it the "Third Platform."

The CRM software we remember installing on user machines is gone; replaced by solutions on a hosted cloud. From there, vendors keep it updated and companies manage software and upgrades simultaneously for all users. Users leverage their devices to access information from anywhere, including their technology-enabled vehicles. Marketing can now access data and make decisions not just based on responses to campaigns and advertisement, but on sentiment, feedback and live customer intelligence and interactions as they are happening in social media circles.

What we are seeing, is not as much a change in CRM but a growth in the capabilities and channels CRM uses to build relationships and improve the customer experience. The cloud is a more efficient way to manage software solutions and data and centrally manage the business processes that run your business. Mobility is an innovative portable means to access information you can use to learn more about the customer and make better decisions about how to serve them. It is something Delta Airlines realized and put into action by providing it's more than 19,000 flight attendants mobile devices in an effort to improve customer service and facilitate onboard transactions. Social media is yet another channel where we interact with our customers. Social media allows people to meet and talk regardless of where they physically live and work; a limitation they also expect you to remove by listening, acting, engaging, and responding to social media conversations.

Social, mobility, advanced analytics, and cloud improvements do not do away with CRM. They improve and enhance it. They further enable it to do what it is intended to do. Changing its name to Cloud CRM or Social CRM only serves as a descriptive appendage that tells you that the technology vendor is staying up-to-date with the technological, social, and cultural changes. Social CRM is not a new type of CRM. CRM includes the newest way people communicate, and meet, and learn about your company. Eventually, saying CRM is Social will be as redundant as calling the Internet the World Wide Web. The internet certainly is worldwide, but doesn't everyone understand that?

A UNIFIED CUSTOMER STRATEGY CRM SYSTEM

The fundamental questions this book presents are not only about how you use CRM today. They are also about the role CRM technology should play in implementing the Unified Customer Strategy approach presented here. I began this book by saying that CRM is about both the strategy and technology that manages customer relationships. I also told you that CRM is the strategy that helps you build customer relationships with the same thought, structure, and intention as you build personal relationships. It accounts for the way relationships are built through engagement, centricity, service, support, transparency, and experience. Shouldn't CRM technology then mirror that strategy? If CRM is the technology that connects all the other strategies, shouldn't these concepts also be visible from the CRM system you use?

Let's take a look, again, at the seven unified strategies from the technology perspective:

RELATIONSHIP – CRM technology shows you the type of relationship customers have, not only with you but other employees, partners, vendors, and distributors. Information is organized to display these relationships by stage as you nurture them. Insight about the relationship is stored at the contact and company level to allow you to easily access information that helps increase transparency and build trust. You will invest genuinely in these customers. This is your customer diary, and you maintain important information about your expectations for the customer and their expectations of you. In a truly collaborative environment, your peers do the same thing, and you benefit from their insight and perspective on the relationship. At a glance, your company can see valuable information that will help you mitigate perception of risk or imbalance in the benefits of the business relationship.

ENGAGEMENT – CRM technology also lets you see all activity for your customer. Some will be strictly transactional, verifying that the activities that compose a specific business process were completed (like sending an email or scheduling a call). But you can move beyond purely transactional activities and document valuable information you can use later to evaluate the accomplishment of your interactions. Did they induce participation and interlock the customer's attention? Did the customer participate and engage? Are they interested in forming or maintaining a relationship with you? Then, CRM technology integration with the communication channels the customer prefers creates a seamless experience for the customer to engage with you and for you to manage those interactions from one place.

CENTRICITY – CRM technology will customize some of these interactions based on the relationship type and phase. The result is a personalized interaction. You will again take advantage of what the CRM system tells you the customer needs in order to feel appreciated and valued. You use CRM data to personalize the experience to the customer and their needs and you make the experience more engaging. It becomes one more way to make them feel that you are making an investment in the relationship.

SERVICE AND SUPPORT – CRM technology also gives you access to the formal and informal agreement your company has made with the customer. It allows you to review the contracts and service agreements that represent your promises to them. When those agreements are not met, case management technology embedded in CRM allows you to create and track service requests to make things right. Escalation technology tells you when and how someone is handling the request. Thankfully, the right CRM strategy ensured that this CRM system accounts for proactive and reactive ways to serve the customer. It gathers intelligence from the many other interactions with customers to make that experience easy and functional for the customer inquiring about the status of the case.

TRANSPARENCY – CRM technology extends to self-help portals, community portals and forums, and social media environments where you have the opportunity to build transparency through open communications. This is the technology you enabled by listening to the voice of the customer and the voice of the employee. You built the channels customers need to make interacting with you easy. Now you are building trust.

EXPERIENCE – CRM is also the technology your business uses to look across all of your relationships and interactions to evaluate if you are providing the functionality the customer expected, in a way that is accessible and emotionally engaging. Reports and dashboards give you a realistic view of the customer's perception of value, their intentions to stay with you, and the efforts they made to recommend you to others. You know this because you have a CRM system that asks the functionality, accessibility, and emotion questions at every point of interaction with the customer.

Before you dismiss the CRM system I just described as a fantasy, consider that every one of the elements I just described already exist in every major CRM application currently in the market. The difference is that the tool I described does not drive the way you manage customer relationships. Instead, the process of relationship, engagement, centricity, service, support, transparency, and experience tell the tool how to manage information, processes, activity automation, and information gathering (especially around the evaluation of the customer experience). This CRM system powers relationship, engagement, centricity, service, support, transparency and experience as a unified strategy for winning and keeping the right customers, employees, and business partners.

SECTION 9

SPEAKING ABOUT INDUSTRY

CRM IS NOT ALWAYS OUT-OF-THE-BOX. UNDERSTAND THE INVESTMENTS THAT MAKE CRM TOOLS WORK FOR YOU.

cus·tom·ize \ transitive verb \ˈkəs-tə-
ˌmīz\:to build, fit, or alter according to
individual specifications[22]

"Pleasure in the job puts perfection in the work."

- Aristotle

If CRM technology is part of your strategy to serve customers and strengthen your customer relationships, then it is important you consider the investment of making it relevant to how you do business (and the requirements of your industry). The unified customer strategy and the relationship phases are applicable to every industry. How each industry operates to market, sell and support customers is going to be different. You may have to choose a CRM tool pre-designed to support your industry processes or make changes to a commercial CRM tool.

Even though the success of CRM strategies depends on successfully and skillfully managing the customer relationship, the success of your CRM technology initiatives depends greatly on the approval of the people who will use it. Adoption is dependent on the alignment of CRM function with the business processes an industry uses to meet the needs of customers while remaining compliant with regulatory requirements. Many of the CRM tools available can serve as an excellent starting point but may require additional customization to make it applicable to your industry.

The insurance industry is a great example. Insurance providers have specific business processes that add structure to the way they do business. You could implement one of the many commercial CRM solutions available. After adding some customer data, you may be able to almost immediately manage contact and account records, schedule activities, assign resources, manage sales pipeline, and create customer service tickets. However, to use the CRM application to sell insurance, for example, you need the system to support the insurance business. If it cannot do that, then it is not of any good to anyone. In fact, it could potentially slow you down. What will make this CRM solution effective is its ability to facilitate business through the automation and arbitration of the processes applicable to insurance. CRM can manage communication campaigns, but insurance companies need those campaigns to control how people receive them and how they will register for educational events that help them make a decision about the insurance they need. CRM can manage appointment scheduling, but insurance companies need an adequate way to assign agents best trained and certified to sell certain products. CRM can store documents like applications and eligibility forms, but insurance companies need a system that can manage the paramount "started but not completed" application and help get the customer to finish the process. CRM must be about the way the insurance company does business. It must support processes like the proactive review of the customer's first bill, new policy processing, up-sell and cross-sell, first notice of loss, orphaned policyholder assignment, and hundreds of other insurance-specific processes.

BUY IT OR BUILD IT?

Some years back I compared the process of leveraging an out-of-the-box CRM solution to the way a car racing company may use a Formula One chassis to expedite creating a new and more powerful racecar. It is a common practice in the racing industry that saves hundreds of thousands of dollars through the repurposing of car parts. The investment required to build a brand new car is high and wrecking a new racecar is just heartbreaking after you have spent so much time and money to build it from nothing. By leveraging an existing chassis as the foundation, racecar companies directly benefit from the frame and basic functional machinery that make the car operational and focus their investment in building the components specific to their race.

Doing the same thing with CRM technology yields similar benefits to you as you implement CRM technology appropriate to the needs of your industry. Using existing CRM technology allows you to assess your needs and align them with what the CRM application already has as a foundation. You can then use a solution that may already include forty to fifty percent of what you need and quickly adapt elements such as screens, forms, dashboards, reports and similar attributes to meet your requisites.

Even though there are similarities between sales, marketing, and support (regardless of the product or service you sell), there will be changes to the interface and nomenclature of an out-of-the-box CRM solution. These changes may go beyond the basic "face-lift" (minimal changes to field labels, field location, etc.). These are details relevant specifically to your industry and sub-specialties within that industry. The extent of the changes will vary from one industry to the next. It could be as simple as changing certain naming conventions (such as from "contact" to "client" or "constituent") or as complicated as changing the solution to fit the various processes that run your business. In any case, these changes must always reflect the way you will use and navigate what will become "your" Formula One racecar.

The extent of the changes will vary by industry and may not always be obvious. Financial Services firms may need customer information to be arranged based on client status. Pharmaceutical sales reps that travel a lot from one physician's office to another may need fields arranged in a way that makes it easy to enter data while they are on the road. Law firms may need to simplify general information screens to make it easier for attorneys to share their Rolodex with the rest of the firm and later find contact information readily in the database of firm clients. How you need to see and access information will determine the changes you make.

There are many industry-specific online forums where you can interact with people ready to share their experiences. Such is the case with a recent online forum for automotive dealerships that illustrate this point very well. The site was created specifically for car dealers as a forum to determine the best type of automotive CRM solutions. The forum, while open to the public, warns vendors not to "spam the thread" with comments about how their CRM solution fits perfectly into the dealer management world. With the clear "don't give us your vision" message to vendors, the forum opens the door for dealers to express their needs and the value they would get from specific features in a CRM solution. Because the forum is open to customers wanting to provide feedback about their car-buying experience, the feedback includes a very useful and unbiased view of what CRM in this industry should accomplish for both the auto dealers and the consumer.

MORE THAN A FACE-LIFT

For a CRM system to work within an industry, it must first fit your culture. Financial advisors, accountants, lawyers, architects, and entertainment agents all have their own way of conducting business within their trade. You have to integrate these cultural nuances and behavior into the functionality of the CRM application. Otherwise, it will be more difficult, maybe impossible, for you to use it and make it applicable to the way you interact with your customers. In some cases, you may find a vendor that has made an investment in your industry and may have already overcome those cultural differences and delivered a product recognized and customized for your market. When that is not the case, and you have to take on these adaptations and customizations on your own, you will need to consider some things. The next few pages will help you determine if an industry-specific solution is the best fit, or if you should use a foundation solution and build from there.

WHO IS YOUR CUSTOMER?

Clients, constituents, franchisees, patients… companies have different names for their customers. Those customers could be individual consumers or companies, or both. Many CRM solutions start as an account-centric (company-centric) tool, which is very different from a contact management solution (that stores contact data without associating the people that work for the same company). While the account-centric approach is advantageous for most companies, it presents a challenge for others.

Consider that in a business environment where the "customer" could be either a company or person, a company-centric system will require that you define how you organize information to fit the way you best do business. The concepts of "account management" and "primary contact relationships" may need to be redefined to accommodate this dynamic. Carefully assess the dynamic of your customer's customers (and do not forget their partners and suppliers). It is common for a solution to accommodate a business easily with consumers, but not a model like that of a franchise. In this model, franchise owners are your customers, but your franchises have customers (end customers,) which you also need to account for in the CRM system.

PRODUCTS OR SERVICES?

It is a grave error to approach the sales cycle and opportunity management process of any organization strictly based on the existing model of the CRM technology you are buying. Opportunity management modules available in most CRM tools are an excellent foundation and powerful for companies that follow a conventional sales cycle that progresses from lead generation to product sale, and ultimately to service and support. In this model, a product is priced (sometimes configured), then quoted, and then invoiced. This is not always the model companies follow, and not at all the pattern for organizations that sell a service.

For companies that sell services, estimating the value of an opportunity is calculated in ways not always supported (and often considered "non-traditional") by many CRM systems. Companies that sell services and have to manage people, time and projects in CRM may find it challenging to use existing CRM solutions without adding solutions and plugins that extend CRM's functionality. Expect some integration to other business-essential data that may be stored in litigation, point-of-sales, point-of-service, or e-commerce systems. It is an area where vendors that offer "all-in-one" solutions have an enormous advantage and may offer the best value. Assessing the ROI of building utilities and tools that take CRM the rest of the way you need it to go must weigh heavily on your decision to select the right CRM tool.

SECTION 10

SPEAKING ABOUT THE JOURNEY

CRM IS A JOURNEY THAT WILL REQUIRE YOUR COMMITMENT AND DEDICATION.

en·deav·or \ verb \in-'de-vər\ : to seriously
or continually try to do (something)[23]

"Perseverance is failing 19 times and succeeding the 20th."

- Julie Andrews

The story I shared at the beginning of the book, sadly, is true. The company referenced is no longer in business. The people in that conference room did not part ways amicably, and they did not leave the experience behind as "just business." Real people were hurt emotionally and financially as the result of that event. The customer lost their trust in the CRM process and the project team, and the CRM corporate sponsor lost her job. The most tragic part of this story is that there was a tremendous opportunity to use this experience to learn to collaborate in other aspects of the business (a problem that attributed to the demise of the company).

TOYS NOT INCLUDED

A while back I was asked what I thought was the toughest challenge to overcome when introducing CRM to a company. I thought for a moment about things like value proposition and convincing salespeople to share their contacts. After seriously thinking about it, I am compelled to answer that the toughest conversation I have with my customers is around the impact of CRM on their business. While ROI and CRM tool selection and deployment are usually the first topics to emerge, discussing that CRM is for everyone in the company (not just sales, or marketing or customer service) has always been the most challenging topic to confront. That's because to many companies the idea of everyone having access to CRM translates to paying for more licenses or including additional stakeholders who may not be completely on board with the concept. Both of these objections immediately reveal that many companies see CRM as either "the tool" or the "thing" sales use to manage customers.

Engaging in the "company-wide CRM" conversation makes business sense. It forces people to think about CRM as a strategic initiative; one that carefully orchestrates plans and methods for winning and retaining customers. CRM is more than the tool we use to manage the customer lifecycle. It is a vehicle to connect all the people in your company with the vision of improving the central relationships of your business through meaningful interactions. When you define it that way, CRM must be used by everyone who contributes to the customer relationship, even if the CRM tool itself is deployed in phases.

Approaching CRM as the exclusive project for a single organization (usually sales, marketing, or support) is common but ineffective for all the reasons we already discussed. A sales or support organization, for example, (at law firms it is usually marketing) may sell their corporate sponsor on the need to implement CRM independently to secure funding for the project. In a tight economy, it is easier to get funding for CRM for one function and then progressively bring in other organizations (maybe even have each organization fund their effort). The approach resembles buying a set of batteries for your kids for Christmas with a note on it that says, "toys not included" (from one of my favorite Bernard Manning quotes). You simply cannot expect independently to implement an initiative that affects the entire business. Regardless of how you deploy the tool, you have to sell corporate sponsors on the value of CRM as a company-wide initiative that deploys a common CRM vision and technology strategy to support EVERY organization. Think "corporate" initiative from the beginning. Do not neglect the strategic conversation that paints the picture of what CRM will mean to everyone. Get consensus even if every group isn't ready or does not have a budget for a company-wide technology implementation.

BUILDING THE RELATIONSHIPS THAT BUILD YOUR BUSINESS

My nine-year-old daughter, Addie, is truly her father's daughter. When I tell people what I do, and she is close enough to hear the conversation, she precariously follows my introduction of the term "CRM" with, "that means Customer Relationship Management." That is amazing to me because of a couple of curious facts: first, she is only nine and second, many of my customers get the acronym wrong. What amazes me most about Addie's understanding of my job is that, despite her finite grasp of what CRM is, she knows that her daddy helps people with their relationships.

I have worked at CRM software companies several times in

my career. It is how I got started in CRM. As I began to work with partner channels, where our attention was more focused on industry solutions (and I emphasize solutions because that is what they are; not accelerators), my focus began to shift away from the technology and steadily towards the people my customers were serving. Not just towards their customers, but towards all the people who help win and keep customers and make them feel rewarded for doing business with them. The guiding principal that CRM is about relationships slowly overpowered the "relational" mentality of connected tables and metadata.

After so many years working on the technology side of CRM, it is easy to let my mind think about technology first. I had to change my mindset to thinking about the result rather than the tools used to get there. The classic "Marketing Myopia" 1960 article quote by Theodore Levitt, "People don't buy quarter inch drills, they buy quarter inch holes," is equally applicable to CRM technology. You are not buying a CRM tool. You are buying a means to stronger customer relationships and customer experiences. You are buying tools to improve knowledge of the customer and (dare I say it), customer intimacy. Technologist and CRM system implementers should never lose sight of that. Just as a fire extinguisher manufacturer knows their business is fighting fires, and pharmaceutical companies know their mandate is to heal people and give them a better standard of living, we should be about the business of helping people build the relationships that build their business.

No effort is more worthy than that which improves the quality of the life of another. No effort deserves more respect that the endeavor of engaging another human being for being of service to them. It is easy to be overwhelmed by the daily toil of work and the sometimes unreasonable expectations of people outside and inside our companies. It makes it easy to forget that the business processes we follow are not there just to help us make money. They are there to guide us through the process of building relationships and assess the level of interaction and engagement we should have with someone in order to guide that relationship. When salespeople reach out to a prospect, it is easy to allow sales quota to drive behavior (especially at the end of the quarter). Nevertheless, salespeople are not just selling, they are providing solutions to problems, and CRM helps them focus on building relationships that make people feel that they are making the right decisions.

Marketing people have the difficult task of educating customers about your brand. Market competition and the increase in consumer knowledge about you and your competitors make it hard for marketing people to use the right methods and effectively use marketing lists, campaigns, and product marketing strategies. CRM ensures that customers appropriately perceive their interactions with marketing as sincere efforts to educate and help. When CRM does not effectively help marketing, customers receive duplicate correspondence, unwanted calls, and existing customers are sold products and services they already have. And although customers at-large know that this type of thing happens, deep down when they receive marketing that is misdirected or undermines your relationship with them, they really feel like you do not care about them or know them as you should.

When people do not get a certain level of empathy from customer service agents, they remember your lack of service and your failure to treat them as someone who should come first. Likewise, when Heather from Geico ends her call with me with "thank you for being our customer for the past 10 years," she is leveraging CRM to show me that longevity in our business relationship is something her company values.

A FINAL WORD OF ENCOURAGEMENT

Since 2004, the New York Times has written a number of stories about military veterans who could not receive their pensions because of the lack of adequate customer relationship and customer engagement processes and systems. One particular story tells us about Doris Hink, the widow of a World War II veteran who had to wait nearly two years to process her claim for a survivor's pension, forcing her daughter to take $12,000 from savings to pay nursing home bills. A December 20, 2012, Daily Beast article reports that in the fiscal year that ended in September, the Department of Veteran Affairs paid $437 million in retroactive benefits to the survivors of nearly 19,500 veterans who died waiting. The legal battle continues as I write this.

The CRM endeavor is not simply a means to manage information about people. It is a worthy endeavor that, when implemented successfully, can improve the lives of the people we serve. The CRM mandate is a call for each of you to acknowledge the value of a strategy that helps you be more accountable to the customers you serve as much as the people who make customers feel rewarded for doing business with you. CRM is about people and building genuine relationships with them, and its benefits can truly help make a difference that can also affect your life in a positive way.

There are moments of exuberance and joy in my job when the faces of my customer's customer are people whose quality of life will improve because of this thing we call CRM. Of equal enjoyment are those moments when people "get it" and we celebrate together the successful completion of a CRM strategic or technology effort. Not because it is so rare to see CRM efforts succeed, but because I know that with the right focus, every CRM initiative can be a successful enterprise.

May this book be of enrichment to your business, and may you find in its pages something that changes your own life, as well, for the best.

I wish you the greatest of success!

References

- [1] Merriam-Webster Dictionary

- [2] Merriam-Webster Dictionary

- [3] Merriam-Webster Dictionary

- [4] Merriam-Webster Dictionary

- [5] WEBER, Craig (2013). "Conversational Capacity: The Secret to Building Successful Teams That Perform When the Pressure Is On Merriam-Webster Dictionary". McGraw-Hill.

- [6] RITTEL, Horst, WEBBER, Melvyn (1969). "Dilemmas in a General Theory of Planning. Panel on Policy Sciences, American Association for the Advancement of Science".

- [7] FARREL, Michael (2003). "Collaborative Circles: Friendship Dynamics and Creative Work". Farrell. University of Chicago Press.

- [8] PAINE, Christopher E.; COCHRAN, Thomas B.; NORRIS, Robert S. (1996). "The Arsenals of the Nuclear Weapons Powers: An Overview". Natural Resources Defense Council.

- [9] MANNING, Harley; BODINE, Kerry; BERNOFF, Josh (2012). Outside In: The Power of Putting Customers at the Center of Your Business". New Harvest.

- [10] Merriam-Webster Dictionary

- [11] Merriam-Webster Dictionary

- [12] SANDERS, Tm (2003). "Love Is the Killer App: How to Win Business and Influence Friends". Crown Business.

- [13] LEVINGER, George; RAUSH, Harold (1977). Close Relationships: Perspectives on the Meaning of Intimacy".

- [14] Merriam-Webster Dictionary

- [15] SEARCY, Tom (2009). "RFPs Suck! How to Master the RFP System Once and for All to Win Big Business". Channel V Books

- [16] DEGREGOR, Dennison (2010). "The Customer- Transparent Enterprise: How Market Leaders are Using 21st Century Customer Transparency to Close the Brand/Customer Gap and Win the Customer Loyalty Wars". Motivational Press.

- [17] Merriam-Webster Dictionary

- [18] LEBOEUF, Michael (2000). "How to Win Customers and Keep Them for Life". Berkley Trade.

- [19] Merriam-Webster Dictionary

- [20] ANDERSON, E. W.; FORNELL, C. (1994). "A customer satisfaction research prospective". In R.T. Rust & R. L. Oliver

- [21] Merriam-Webster Dictionary

- [22] Merriam-Webster Dictionary

- [23] Merriam-Webster Dictionary